Sarah Mayor

THE FARMHOUSE COOKBOOK

Photography by Andrew Montgomery

QUADRILLE

Contents

The cookbook in your hands is one very much rooted in a place. That place is the Yeo Valley, a beautiful part of Somerset, which lies between the Mendip Hills and the Chew Valley in the UK, and is where I grew up and live today. Dad's family have been farming here in the West Country since the days of the 15th century and he and Mom bought our farm on the edge of Blagdon Lake in 1961.

Food has always been a huge part of my life. Well, when you're surrounded by such amazing produce—fruit, vegetables, fish, wonderful meat, and dairy—it's hard to not to be inspired to cook. And so from a young age, if I wasn't helping to look after the calves, or dangling worms into the pond in hope of trout, I'd be busy in the kitchen helping Mom.

This makes it all sound rather idyllic. Well in some ways I suppose it was. But it was also ruddy hard work. From a young age it was all hands on deck, for me and for my brother Tim and sister Amanda. We'd help with everything: feeding the cows, lambing, calving, not to mention the enviable task of mucking out. Always a favorite!

At the time, and this would have been the mid-Sixties, we had all sorts of animals: cows, sheep, ponies, chickens, turkeys. A few years after that, we started growing potatoes, corn, and strawberries, and started a "pick your own" business. Visitors were always saying how they loved our picturesque spot in the valley by the lake, so we decided to set up a tea room serving scones and jam and lovely clotted cream made from our own milk. Soon we had queues stretching right up to the main road!

But making lots of clotted cream left us with a problem: what to do with all the lowfat milk we had left over. Then Dad had the genius idea of making yogurt. I say "genius idea." Actually, at the time, it seemed a bit bonkers. You have to remember that these were days before you could pick up things like lemongrass and pomegranates from your local grocery store or supermarket. These were days before grocery stores or supermarkets period. Put it this way: at the time, olive oil was considered exotic. Our first yogurt contract wasn't even with a store; it was with a Bristol hospital!

Thankfully, Dad's energy, drive, and foresight paid off. There was a massive food revolution in this country and people started to realize that yogurt wasn't just good for you—it was delicious, too. Gradually it became the center of the family farm, and we haven't looked back since.

It wasn't just Dad who was being inspired by this revolution in food; I was, too. By this time, I was a fully fledged, card-carrying foodie. I had learned so much from my life on the farm, but I was hungry for more. So in 1979, I traded my beloved West Country for London and a career in catering, though it wasn't long before I was lured back to Somerset, where I settled down to have my three children. When the youngest had reached school age, a friend of mine asked me if I might want to teach at her cookery school, The Grange. I'd never taught before, so I was a little, how shall we say, hesitant? Well, she twisted my arm, and I'm really glad she did. The students were fantastic and I thoroughly enjoyed sharing my skills and encouraging them to use their senses: to smell, to touch, to taste. To think about seasonality, about where their food comes from and, in the case of meat, how the animal has been raised. It was also great for me to be able to share my love of the social side of food, the joy—and importance—of sitting around with family and friends to share a wonderful meal.

It's funny, lots of things don't seem to have
changed that much over the years. Yes, the farm
is much bigger these days, but the same things that
were important then are important now. As a family,
we still all live within about six miles of each
other. My brother Tim, who runs Yeo Valley,
lives in the house we grew up in. Mom lives in
a village just down the road. I'm a stone's throw
away on my own organic farm and my sister, Amanda,
is just a short drive from us. We're all still
very involved in Yeo Valley, just as we always
have been. And good food, made with local, seasonal
ingredients, is as important to us as it ever was.

We now have a fantastic restaurant at our HQ, which
is open to the people who work for Yeo Valley and
anyone who comes to use our spaces for conferences
and that sort of thing. For me to have had the
opportunity to bring everything I learned in my
cooking career back to the farm has been incredibly
satisfying, and not something I ever imagined would
happen. I've very much enjoyed planning a whole
year's worth of seasonal menus for our kitchens,
all of which make full use of the lovely organic
produce from our gardens, farm, and dairy.

On the following pages are some of my absolute
favorite recipes, all of them inspired by my
surroundings and my journey as a cook. I'd describe
them as classic British farmhouse dishes with
a modern twist. Some are things we cook in our
restaurant and our tea rooms; others are based
on meals we enjoyed as children. The rest are
dishes we like to eat at home when spending time
with family and friends. We're a big family—
9 grandchildren at the last count—and this
is family food; food to eat together. I've had
a fantastic year of cooking, tasting, and tweaking.
I very much hope you enjoy the results.

From pasture to pot

Somerset has a fantastic climate for growing grass. So, if you're a farmer who lives here, the sensible thing to do is to keep dairy cows. All ours are British Friesians: they're a hardy breed that thrives on lush pastures.

Our Lakemead pedigree herd, which is 400-strong, is divided across two farms. One is here at Holt Farm, on the edge of Blagdon Lake in the Yeo Valley; the other is at Yoxter Farm, four miles away up on the Mendips.

We make it in pretty much the same way. We add a type of good bacteria to warm milk, the bacteria eat the lactose, and this makes lactic acid, which protects the milk from harmful bacteria. It's a little bit like the pickling process. Fancy making yogurt yourself? Turn to page 14 for an easy recipe.

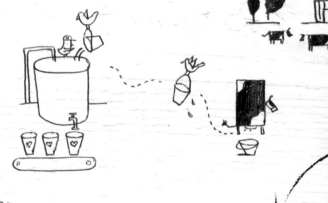

Yogurt was invented as a way to preserve milk, which goes off quickly in warm climates. People found that by adding special bacteria, they could help milk keep for much longer. Ingenious!

Our cows graze on clover-rich grass in the warmer months and then, when it gets a bit cooler, we bring them inside. They have well-ventilated, spacious housing with comfy bedding and plenty of organic winter feed known as silage—a type of pickled grass. We also give them cereals like wheat, barley, and triticale. Eating a balanced diet isn't just important for humans!

We have a special and rather large barn, where we rear our calves—up to 400 a year. There's a huge demand for the best of our male calves, which are sold for breeding all over the world. The rest we rear for beef. All the females go back into our milking herd.

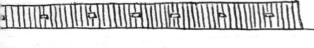

Our cows amble into the dairy twice a day for milking, where they each give around 5.5 gl [25 L] per day. It takes us three hours to milk 200 cows. And the milk doesn't have far to travel; the place where we make our yogurt is just half a mile away.

We have nine staff looking after the cows, as well as a conservation team, who spend their days dry stone walling, planting trees, and keeping the hedges in order. They also look after the Miscanthus, a special type of grass that we use to fuel the biomass boiler, which heats our HQ.

the dairy

Now, this probably won't come as a huge surprise, but we think milk's magical stuff. One little fact we like to recount is that baby blue whales can live for up to five years on their mother's milk alone—it really is packed with goodness. And so versatile! Some good creamy yogurt with granola for breakfast; a blob of crème fraîche stirred through ribbons of fresh pasta for lunch; a piece of fennel and chili butter on a nice, rare steak for supper. Glorious.

Mom and Margot get ready for the cameras

Our parents set up the farm back in the Sixties, and cows have been part of the family ever since.

Felicity

We're huge fans of the British Friesian cow, a sturdy breed that thrives on our clover-rich grass.

In the winter, our cows live indoors in the warm where they eat a balanced diet of silage (pickled grass) and grains.

We give each cow their own special mix, depending on which nutrients they need. Talk about individual treatment!

They even have special robotic scrapey things in their quarters which keep things tidy. A nice, clean floor helps make sure their feet stay dry and healthy.

The DIY Dairy

There's a certain smug satisfaction to be had by making things like yogurt from scratch. And it really doesn't have to be complicated, as these recipes show...

Yogurt

This won't be as thick as store-bought yogurt but if you want it a little thicker, simply tip it into a cheesecloth-lined strainer and let it drain in the refrigerator for an hour or two until it's a consistency that you like.

Yogurt cheese

This is similar to fresh cream cheese and is made simply by draining plain yogurt overnight to rid it of all its liquid. Rolled into balls and preserved in oil with herbs and other flavorings, these are lovely served with crackers, and maybe a dab of tapenade, basil pesto, or sundried tomato pesto. They'll keep for a good week in the refrigerator.

Put 4½ cups [1 L] whole milk into a pan and heat it to 185°F [85°C]. It will be steaming and bubbles will appear around the edge of the pan. Pour it into a very clean bowl and let cool to 109 to 115°F [43 to 46°C], then whisk in ¼ cup [65 g] plain yogurt with live active cultures. You now need to keep the mixture warm and undisturbed for a minimum of 7 to 12 hours to thicken (we like to either pour ours into a thermos flask or wrap it in a clean towel and leave it somewhere warm like the airing cupboard, near the Aga, or by a radiator). Stir the yogurt well and pour into suitable refrigerator-size pots with lids. Chill overnight in the refrigerator, during which time the yogurt will thicken even more.

MAKES 4½ CUPS [1 L]

Mix 6½ cups [1.5 L] Greek-style plain yogurt with 2 tsp salt. Spoon it into a large strainer lined with a large square of double-thick cheesecloth. Tie the opposite corners of the cheesecloth together, suspend it over the bowl, and let drain in the refrigerator until it stops dripping—about 48 hours. Remove the yogurt cheese from the cheesecloth and discard the whey. Roll the cheese into 35 x 1-oz [25-g] golf-size balls, and pop them into a sterilized preserving jar with either some fresh herbs, peeled garlic cloves, strips of pared lemon zest, cracked black peppercorns, crushed or whole dried chiles, or a combination of whichever you fancy. Pour extra-virgin olive oil over the cheese to cover, and seal. Leave for 24 hours before serving.

MAKES APPROX. 2 LB [900 G] (35 BALLS)

Why not try ...?

Using your yogurt to make a spicy feta and roasted red pepper dip

Preheat the oven to 425°F [220°C]. Rub a red bell pepper and a chile with a little olive oil, put them in a small roasting pan, and roast for 25 minutes until their skins have blackened. Remove from the oven, seal in a plastic bag, and let cool, then remove the skin, seeds, and stalks, setting the flesh aside. Pop into a food processor with 7 oz [200 g] feta cheese, 4 to 5 Tbsp Greek-style yogurt, and 1 Tbsp extra-virgin olive oil and blend into a coarse paste.

Or how about ...?

Instead of preserving the cheese in oil, try serving it as a dip sprinkled with herbs and olive oil or a North African spice blend called *Za'atar*, a mixture of toasted sesame seeds, a thymelike herb, sumac, and salt.

Ricotta

You can make ricotta using liquid rennet, distilled vinegar, white wine vinegar, and even yogurt, but we think this recipe —which uses lemon juice—gives the right combination of taste and consistency. The longer you let the ricotta drain the firmer it will become. After 8 minutes the curds are soft and can be eaten just as they are. After 20 minutes they'll have become firm enough to hold their shape but will still be soft. From between 40 and 60 minutes they will be solid enough to cook with. Whatever you do, be sure to use the freshest milk you can lay your hands on—you'll taste the difference.

Line a large strainer with a layer of damp fine cheesecloth. Put 1.9 qt [2.25 L] whole milk, in a pan with 1 cup [250 ml] heavy cream and ½ tsp salt, place over medium-low heat, and heat slowly to 199°F [93°C], stirring gently occasionally. When it reaches the right temperature the milk will be steaming, the surface will be shimmering, and small bubbles will have appeared on the surface. Whip the pan off the heat and stir in 4 Tbsp freshly squeezed lemon juice for a few seconds until curds start to form. Leave undisturbed for 2 minutes then, using a slotted spoon, gently ladle the curds into the strainer, taking care not to break them up. Drain until the ricotta reaches the desired consistency (see left). Cover and refrigerate for up to 2 days.

MAKES APPROX. 1¼ LB [600 G]

Why not try....? Baked ricotta with thyme
Preheat the oven to 350°F [180°C]. Line 4 to 6 new 3- to 3½-in [8- to 9-cm] terracotta flowerpots with parchment paper. Mix 1½ cups [350 g] ricotta with 3 large egg yolks, 1 Tbsp chopped thyme leaves, grated zest of 1 small lemon, ⅓ cup [25 g] finely grated Parmesan, and season. Whisk 3 egg whites into soft peaks and gently fold in. Spoon into the pots and bake for 20 to 25 minutes until puffed up and golden. Serve with toasted bread.

Butter

This butter is deliciously sweet and so much nicer than most of the butter you can find in the stores. The leftover buttermilk isn't quite the same as the cultured stuff that you can buy, but it's still great for making bread.

Put 2½ cups [600 ml] heavy cream **and** ¼ tsp salt (if you like your butter salted) into a food processor and blend until it thickens and separates into butter and buttermilk. **Add** 4 to 5 Tbsp ice-cold water and continue to process until the butter starts to form into small lumps. Tip the mixture into a strainer set over a bowl to save the buttermilk. This can be chilled for up to 2 days. Put the butter onto a plate and press it with the back of a fork to squeeze out all the excess buttermilk. Gradually it will come together into a ball with no signs of any liquid seeping out. Shape into blocks or balls or press into small pots, cover, and chill until needed. This will keep in the refrigerator for up to 5 days.

MAKES APPROX. 10 OZ [280 G]

Or how about ...?

Flavored butter.
Mix 7 Tbsp [100 g] of the soft butter with ¼ tsp salt, some freshly ground black pepper, and your choice of flavoring (see below). Spoon the butter onto a sheet of plastic wrap, wax paper, or nonstick parchment paper and shape into a 1¼-in [3-cm] wide roll. Wrap up tightly and chill until firm.

1. Fennel seed, chile & garlic— 1 tsp crushed fennel seeds, ½ minced chile, ¼ tsp crushed dried chiles, and 2 crushed garlic cloves. 2. Blue cheese— 1¾ oz [50 g] rich buttery blue cheese and 1 tsp chopped thyme leaves. 3. Sundried tomato, rosemary & olive— ½ oz [15 g] each of finely chopped sundried tomatoes and pitted black olives, 1 small crushed garlic clove, and 1 tsp minced rosemary. 4. Tarragon & garlic— 2 Tbsp chopped tarragon and 2 crushed garlic cloves.

Cream cheese

To make a firmer cheese that you can slice, wrap the curds tightly in the cheesecloth and refrigerate overnight.

Put 4½ cups [1 L] whole milk into a pan and warm it gently until it reaches 99°F [37°C]. Pour into a bowl, stir in 5 tsp rennet and leave somewhere cool (but not in the refrigerator) for 2 hours or until set. Then break up the curds with a fork and stir in ¾ tsp salt. Line a large strainer with a double sheet of cheesecloth, rest it over a bowl, and pour in the cheesy curds. Cover and leave somewhere cool (but again, not the refrigerator) overnight.

MAKES APPROX. 7 OZ [200 G]

Why not try ...?
Cream cheese hearts with vanilla sugar

Line 6 heart-shaped coeur à la crème molds with damp cheesecloth and place on a rack over a small roasting pan. Press ⅞ cup [200 g] cream cheese through a strainer into a mixing bowl. Lightly whip 1 cup [225 ml] heavy cream with 2 Tbsp superfine sugar until it just starts to form soft peaks then gently fold it into the cream cheese. Spoon into the prepared molds, cover, and chill for 2 hours. Turn out onto small plates and serve sprinkled with a little vanilla sugar (either prebought or made by mixing the seeds from 1 vanilla bean into ¼ cup [50 g] sifted superfine sugar) and some chilled pouring cream.

Crème fraîche

Homemade crème fraîche has a wonderful texture and flavor. If you find yourself wanting to make a second lot, set aside a few Tbsp from the first batch and use that instead of the buttermilk. The results will be thicker and even more delicious.

Pour ⅞ cup [200 ml] heavy cream into a small mixing bowl and stir in 2 Tbsp cultured buttermilk. Cover with plastic wrap and leave in a warm room for 24 hours. After that, the mixture should have thickened and taken on a pleasant sour flavor. Cover and chill until needed, during which time it will thicken to the perfect texture. It will keep in the refrigerator for up to 1 week.

MAKES APPROX. 9 OZ [250 G]

Now try ...
Tagliatelle with crème fraîche, butter & cheese

Mix 1 cup [250 ml] crème fraîche with 4 large free-range egg yolks, scant 1 cup [75 g] finely grated Parmesan, and some salt and pepper. Toss together with 1 lb 2 oz [500 g] cooked, drained egg tagliatelle and 2 Tbsp [30 g] unsalted butter over low heat for 1 minute until the sauce has thickened, then serve with grated Parmesan.

Clotted cream

Clotted cream is a very British variety of heavy cream — super thick and traditionally served with scones. This homemade version is delicious with desserts and will keep for up to 5 days in the refrigerator.

Preheat the oven to 176°F [80°C]. Pour 2½ cups [600 ml] heavy cream into a 11-by-7-in [28-by-18-cm] shallow ceramic baking dish and cover tightly with foil, then bake the cream for 10 to 12 hours or overnight until the top forms a thick, pale-yellow crust and the rest of the cream underneath has reduced and thickened slightly. Let cool, then cover with plastic wrap and chill for 8 hours or overnight. To use, scoop off the thick cream on top (this is the clotted cream). The remaining thinner cream can be used in ordinary cooking.

MAKES APPROX. 10½ OZ [300 G]

Now why not try ...?
Clotted cream ice cream Put 2½ cups [600 ml] whole milk and 1 cup [225 g] clotted cream into a nonstick pan. Scrape out the seeds from 1 vanilla bean, add the bean and seeds to the pan, and bring to a boil. Let infuse for 20 minutes. Whisk 6 large egg yolks and scant 1 cup [175 g] superfine sugar together in a bowl until pale and thick. Return the milk to a boil, then remove the vanilla bean and stir into the egg yolks. Strain into the cleaned-out pan and cook over gentle heat, stirring, until the mix has thickened and lightly coats the back of a wooden spoon. Pour back into the bowl and let cool, then cover and chill overnight. The next day churn the mixture in an ice-cream maker. Spoon into a plastic container, cover, and freeze until needed.

Milk shakes

The thing to bear in mind here is that the creamier the milk and the other ingredients, the richer and more unctuous the shake will be. We make ours with Greek-style or whole yogurt or, if we really want to push the boat out, a good ice cream. Here are four of our favorite combinations. All you need to do is blitz the ingredients together with a few ice cubes.

Strawberry—1 cup [250 ml] ice-cold whole milk, 3½ oz [100 g] vanilla ice cream or plain or strawberry yogurt, 1¾ cups [250 g] berries, and 1 Tbsp honey if needed.

Chocolate—1 cup [250 ml] ice-cold whole milk, 3½ oz [100 g] vanilla ice-cream or whole plain yogurt, 1 oz [25 g] optional piece of homemade honeycomb (see page 63), and 7 Tbsp [100 g] chocolate spread or chocolate and nut spread.

Banana—1 cup [250 ml] ice-cold whole milk, 3½ oz [100 g] ripe peeled banana, 3½ oz [100 g] vanilla ice cream, or whole plain yogurt, 1 Tbsp maple syrup if needed, and 1 tsp vanilla bean paste or extract.

Peanut butter—1 cup [250 ml] ice-cold whole milk, 3½ oz [100 g] vanilla ice cream or whole plain yogurt, 7 Tbsp [100 g] smooth organic peanut butter with no added sugar, and 1 Tbsp honey or agave syrup if needed.

MAKES 1 REALLY LARGE GLASS (or a bottle)

It's recipes like this that make us rejoice in finding a few spare lumps of stilton at the back of the refrigerator. Within a few minutes you can have a rich and creamy soup on the table. If you're not in the mood for making the scones, crusty bread never disappoints.

Celery & stilton soup with hot potato scones

SERVES 4 TO 6

3 Tbsp [40 g] butter

1 large onion, chopped

10½ oz [300 g] celery stalks, thinly sliced

2 Tbsp all-purpose flour

3 cups [750 ml] good chicken broth

4¼ oz [125 g] derinded creamy blue cheese, such as Colston Bassett stilton, crumbled

⅓ cup [80 ml] light cream

Chopped chives to garnish

Salt and freshly ground black pepper

FOR THE POTATO SCONES:

3½ oz [100 g] mealy potatoes, peeled and cut into chunks

1½ cups [175 g] all-purpose flour, plus extra for rolling out

1 Tbsp baking powder

3½ Tbsp [50 g] chilled butter, cut into pieces

¼ cup [60 ml] whole milk

1. Melt the butter in a large pan, add the onion and celery, cover, and cook over low heat for 20 minutes until really soft but not colored. Stir in the flour and cook gently for 1 minute, then gradually stir in the stock and bring to a boil. Cover and let simmer for 20 minutes.

2. Meanwhile, make the scones. Preheat the oven to 425°F [220°C]. Tip the potatoes into a pan of well-salted water, bring to a boil, and simmer for 15 minutes or until tender. Drain and leave for the steam to die down, then mash and let cool.

3. Sift the flour, baking powder, and a large pinch of salt into a food processor, add the butter, and whiz until it resembles bread crumbs. Add the potatoes and whiz together briefly, then tip into a mixing bowl and stir in the milk to form a soft dough. Turn the dough out onto a floured counter and knead very lightly into a ball, then roll out to a thickness of ¾ in [2 cm] and cut into 2½-in [6-cm] circles, rekneading and rolling out the trimmings to make 6 small scones. Pop them, slightly apart, on a lightly floured baking sheet and bake for about 10 minutes until risen and golden brown.

4. Let the soup cool for a few minutes, then blend in batches until smooth. Strain the soup, pour about 2 cups [500 ml] into the blender, add the cheese, and blend until smooth again. Stir back into the remaining soup with the cream and some seasoning and reheat gently. Ladle into warmed bowls, garnish with chopped chives, and serve with the hot buttered scones.

You can make this recipe with store-bought ricotta and it will be great. But, if you do like the idea of making your own, your efforts won't go unnoticed. The results will be fabulous. Our recipe for it is on page 16.

Swiss chard, ricotta & lemon cannelloni

SERVES 6

FOR THE TOMATO SAUCE:

1 small onion, quartered

1 small carrot, cut into coarse chunks

1 celery stalk, cut into coarse chunks

1½ Tbsp olive oil

1¼ lb [600 g] canned chopped tomatoes

3 fresh bay leaves

1 tsp honey

Salt and freshly ground black pepper

FOR THE FILLING:

2 Tbsp [25 g] butter

2¼ lb [1 kg] Swiss chard, stalks discarded and leaves finely shredded

2 garlic cloves, crushed

1 cup [250 g] ricotta (see page 16), well drained

Finely grated zest of 1 large lemon

½ cup plus 2 tsp [50 g] finely grated Parmesan

12 sheets [about 300 g] dried lasagna pasta

1 Tbsp olive oil

FOR THE CHEESE SAUCE:

2½ cups [600 ml] whole milk

¼ cup [65 g] butter

Scant ½ cup [50 g] all-purpose flour

3 Tbsp heavy cream

1⅓ cups [150 g] grated cheddar

1 free-range egg yolk

1. For the tomato sauce: Put the onion, carrot, and celery into a food processor and pulse until finely chopped. Heat the oil in a large pan, add the chopped veg and ¼ tsp of salt, then cover and cook over low heat for 10 minutes, until the veg are soft but not browned. Uncover, add the tomatoes, bay leaves, honey, and 7 Tbsp [100 ml] water and bring to a boil, stirring. Simmer for 1 hour, stirring frequently, or until the sauce is reduced and concentrated. Remove the bay leaves, season to taste, and let cool.

2. For the filling: Heat a small piece of the butter in a pan, then add as much of the chard as you can. Let it wilt down, then add the rest. Cover and cook for 2 to 3 minutes, until tender, then tip into a colander and squeeze out as much liquid as possible. Melt the remaining butter in the pan, add the garlic, and as soon as it starts sizzling, add the chard leaves and stir to mix. Transfer to a bowl and let cool, then stir in the ricotta, zest, and Parmesan and season to taste.

3. Bring a large pan of salted water to a boil. Spoon the tomato sauce over the bottom of a large baking dish. Drop the lasagna sheets one at a time into the boiling water, add the oil, and cook for 12 minutes or until al dente. Drain well, separate, and lay out side by side on plastic wrap. Divide the chard filling between them, spooning it along one short edge of each sheet. Roll them up and place them side by side, seam-side down on top of the tomato sauce.

4. Preheat the oven to 375°F [190°C]. Bring the milk to a boil. Melt the butter in another pan, add the flour, and gently cook for 1 minute, then beat in the milk and simmer for 10 minutes. Set aside, stir in the cream, half the cheese, and egg yolk and some seasoning.

5. Pour the cheese sauce over the top of the cannelloni and sprinkle over the rest of the cheese. Bake for 30 to 35 minutes or until golden and bubbling.

Soufflé recipes are sometimes rather scary. You never quite know whether they're going to rise triumphantly or sink like a stone. Well, no such worries here.

For a change try ...
Serving these soufflés with a salad of sliced tomatoes and chopped fresh herbs like basil, some good olive oil, sea salt, and pepper. Just the thing for a summer's day ...

Twice-baked goat cheese soufflés with radish & watercress salad

SERVES 6

1¼ cups [300 ml] whole milk

1 shallot, sliced

2 bay leaves

6 black peppercorns

3 Tbsp [45 g] butter, plus extra for greasing

¾ cup [65 g] finely grated Parmesan

⅓ cup [40 g] all-purpose flour

¼ tsp cayenne pepper

3 large free-range eggs, separated

3½ oz [100 g] soft rindless goat cheese, crumbled

⅞ cup [200 ml] heavy cream

Salt and freshly ground black pepper

FOR THE SALAD:

½ tsp Dijon mustard

1½ tsp red wine vinegar

2½ Tbsp extra-virgin olive oil

5¼ oz [150 g] mixed watercress sprigs, pea shoots, lamb's lettuce, and baby beet leaves

1 large bunch radishes, trimmed and sliced

1. Bring the milk, shallot, bay leaves, and peppercorns to a boil in a pan. Set aside for 20 to 30 minutes to infuse, then strain, discarding the flavorings.

2. Meanwhile, grease six 4-oz [120-ml] ramekins with butter and coat the insides with ¾ cup [20 g] of the Parmesan.

3. Preheat the oven to 350°F [180°C]. Melt the butter in a nonstick pan, add the flour, and cook gently over low heat for 1 minute. Gradually beat in the milk and bring to a boil, stirring. The mixture will be quite thick. Stir in the cayenne pepper, egg yolks, goat cheese, ½ tsp salt, and some pepper, pour into a large mixing bowl, and let cool slightly.

4. Whisk the egg whites in a clean bowl into soft peaks. Gently fold them into the sauce. Spoon the mix into the ramekins, pop them into a small roasting pan, and pour enough boiling water into the pan to come halfway up their sides. Bake for 16 to 18 minutes, until the soufflés are puffed up and set. Remove the ramekins from the water and let the soufflés sink and cool.

5. To serve: Preheat the oven to 425°F [220°C]. Carefully turn the soufflés out of the ramekins and arrange them upside-down in a large, lightly buttered baking dish. Season the cream to taste and pour over the soufflés, then sprinkle over the remaining grated Parmesan and bake for about 12 minutes until the soufflés have puffed up again and the sauce is golden and bubbling.

6. For the salad: Whisk the mustard and vinegar together in a small bowl, then gradually whisk in the oil and season to taste. Toss the dressing through the leaves and radishes and serve with the hot soufflés.

The thing that really sets this tart apart is the dough, which has a spot of cheddar in it, as well as some oatmeal for a pleasingly nutty bite. As for the filling, any good blue cheese will do.

Blue cheese & leek tart in cheesy oatmeal pastry

SERVES 6 TO 8

FOR THE CHEESY
OATMEAL PIE DOUGH:

1½ cups [175 g] all-purpose flour

Scant 1 cup [65 g] medium oatmeal

Pinch salt

3½ Tbsp [50 g] chilled butter,
cut into small pieces

3½ Tbsp chilled lard,
cut into small pieces

⅔ cup [75 g] finely grated
cheddar

FOR THE FILLING:

¼ cup [65 g] butter

14 oz [400 g] trimmed leeks,
halved lengthwise,
cleaned, and thinly sliced

1¼ cups [300 ml] whipping
or heavy cream

3 extra-large free-range eggs

5¼ oz [150 g] derinded blue
cheese, finely crumbled

1 Tbsp chopped fresh
thyme leaves

Salt and freshly
ground black pepper

1. For the pie dough: Pop the flour into a food processor with the oatmeal, salt, butter, and lard and whiz briefly until the mixture looks like fine bread crumbs. Add the grated cheese and whiz again, then stir in 2 Tbsp of ice-cold water and process very briefly until the mixture comes together in a ball.

2. Thinly roll out the dough and use to line a 10-in [25-cm] loose-bottomed tart pan. Prick the bottom all over with a fork and chill for 20 minutes. Preheat the oven to 400°F [200°C].

3. Line the chilled pastry shell with wax paper and pie weights and bake for 15 to 20 minutes, until the edges of the dough are cookie colored. Remove the paper and weights and return the pan to the oven for 7 to 8 minutes until the base is golden brown. Set aside. Reduce the oven temperature to 375°F [190°C].

4. For the filling: Melt the butter in a large saucepan, add the sliced leeks, and season lightly. Cover and cook gently for a couple of minutes until just softened, then uncover and cook for another 3 to 5 minutes until the leeks are tender and any excess liquid has evaporated. Let cool slightly.

5. Mix the cream and eggs together in a bowl with some salt and pepper to taste. Stir in the leeks, blue cheese, and thyme, then pour the mixture into the tart shell. Cook in the oven for about 30 minutes until just set and lightly browned on top. Let cool slightly before turning out and serving.

Our farm runs alongside Blagdon Lake, which, as well as being beautiful to look at, is absolutely teeming with trout. No surprise then that trout dishes feature rather heavily at home and at our tea rooms.

Deep trout fish cakes with lemon butter & chive sauce

SERVES 4

Three 10½-oz [300-g] trout

3½ Tbsp [50 g] butter, melted

4 scallions, trimmed and thinly sliced

15¾ oz [450 g] mealy potatoes, peeled, cut into chunks, and boiled until tender

2½ Tbsp minced curly leaf parsley

All-purpose flour, for dusting

2 Tbsp sunflower oil

Salt and freshly ground black pepper

FOR THE LEMON BUTTER SAUCE:

2 Tbsp dry white wine

1 Tbsp lemon juice

1 small shallot, minced

1 Tbsp heavy cream

5 Tbsp [75 g] chilled unsalted butter, cut into tiny pieces

1 Tbsp minced chives

1. Preheat the oven to 400°F [200°C]. Brush the trout with half the melted butter and season well. Pop them on a buttered baking sheet and roast for 12 to 15 minutes, until just cooked through. Let cool, then peel back the top layer of skin from each fish and run a knife between the 2 fillets. Carefully ease the fish away from the bones, and flake into small chunky pieces. Let drain on paper towels.

2. Warm the remaining melted butter in a small pan. Add the scallions and cook gently for 1 minute. Set aside. Pop the boiled potatoes into a bowl and mash until smooth, then stir in the scallions, flaked fish, and parsley. Season to taste. Using lightly floured hands, shape the mix into four 2-in [5-cm] thick fish cakes. Cover and chill for at least 1 hour.

3. To cook the fish cakes: Heat the oil in a large frying pan and preheat the oven to 400°F [200°C]. Dust each cake with flour, add to the pan, and cook over medium heat for 3 to 4 minutes on each side until golden brown. Transfer to a greased baking sheet and bake for 12 to 15 minutes until hot all the way through.

4. Meanwhile, make the sauce. Put the wine, lemon juice, shallot, and 3 Tbsp water into a small pan, bring to a boil, and simmer until reduced by half. Strain, return to the pan, and simmer until reduced to 1 Tbsp. Add the cream and simmer for a bit longer, then lower the heat and gradually whisk in the butter until smooth and thick. Stir in the chopped chives and season to taste. Lift the fish cakes onto warmed plates and spoon over a little of the sauce. Serve with some steamed broccoli or spinach.

This is a deliciously simple, clean-tasting cheesecake, which we love to serve with fresh or stewed fruits, as they each come into season. Baked rhubarb and stewed gooseberries are always firm favorites.

Orange yogurt cheese cheesecake

SERVES 12

2 large, juicy navel oranges

2 lb [900 g] Yogurt cheese (see page 14)

1¼ cups [250 g] superfine sugar

3 Tbsp cornstarch

3 extra-large free-range eggs, plus 1 extra yolk

⅞ cup [200 ml] crème fraîche or sour cream

FOR THE BASE:

7 Tbsp [110 g] butter

7 oz [200 g] graham crackers, crushed into fine crumbs

1 Tbsp raw brown sugar

FOR THE TOPPING:

⅝ cup [150 ml] crème fraîche or sour cream

1 tsp superfine sugar

1 tsp lemon juice

1. Preheat the oven to 350°F [180°C]. Line the bottom of a 9½-in [24-cm] clip-sided pan with nonstick parchment paper.

2. For the base: Melt the butter in a medium pan then stir in the cookie crumbs and sugar. Spoon into the pan and press down to form a thin, even layer. Bake for 10 minutes, then remove and let cool. Increase the oven temperature to 475°F [240°C]. Grease the sides of the pan with a little more butter.

3. Finely grate the zest from the oranges and squeeze the juice from 1 of them. Scoop the yogurt cheese into a bowl and beat until smooth and creamy (or use a stand mixer if you have one). Beat in the sugar, cornstarch, three-quarters of the grated zest, and 1 Tbsp of the orange juice, followed by the eggs, one at a time, and then the yolk. Stir in the crème fraîche or sour cream.

4. Pour the cheesecake mixture into the pan and bake for 10 minutes, then lower the oven temperature to 225°F [110°C] and bake for another 35 minutes, or until just set but still quite wobbly in the center. Turn off the oven, leave the door ajar (wedge it open with the handle of wooden spoon if necessary), and let cool inside for about an hour.

5. For the topping: Mix the crème fraîche or sour cream with the sugar and lemon juice. Spread over the top, cover loosely with plastic wrap, and chill for 8 hours or overnight. Just before serving, sprinkle the remaining orange zest over the top.

Caramelized oatmeal, cider & honey creams with blueberries

This is a creamy dessert featuring local brandy but you can replace with Calvados, if you like.

SERVES 4

1 Tbsp [15 g] butter

Scant 1 cup [50 g] coarse oatmeal

2 Tbsp light brown sugar

Scant 1 cup [225 ml] heavy cream

2 Tbsp honey

3½ Tbsp [50 ml] cider brandy or Calvados

1⅓ cups [200 g] fresh blueberries

1. Preheat the oven to 350°F [180°C]. Melt the butter in a small pan, stir in the oatmeal and sugar, and mix together well. Spread the mixture onto a small baking sheet in a thin layer and bake for 12 minutes or until golden brown. Remove and let cool, then crumble into small pieces with your fingers.

2. Whip the cream in a large mixing bowl until it is just beginning to thicken, then whisk in the honey and, gradually, the brandy, until the mixture holds in soft, billowy peaks. Quickly and gently, fold in three-quarters of the caramelized oatmeal and half the blueberries.

3. Drop a large spoonful of the blueberry cream into the bottom of 4 dessert glasses and scatter over half the remaining blueberries and caramelized oatmeal. Repeat once more and serve immediately.

Milk and honey desserts with honeycomb & cream

SERVES 6

1 vanilla bean

2½ cups [600 ml] whole milk

1¼ cups [300 ml] heavy cream

¾ oz [18 g] leaf gelatin

1 jar honeycomb honey

Ice-cold pouring cream, to serve

1. Slit the vanilla bean open lengthwise and scrape out the seeds with the tip of a knife. Put the milk, cream, vanilla seeds, and bean into a pan and bring up to a boil. Set aside for 10 minutes to infuse the milk with the flavor of vanilla, then remove the bean.

2. Meanwhile, put the gelatin into a bowl of cold water and let soak for 5 minutes. Bring the cream almost back to a boil, then remove from the heat. Lift the gelatin out of the water, squeeze out the excess water, and drop it into the hot milk. Stir until dissolved, then stir in ½ cup [150 g] of the honey.

3. Strain the mixture into a pitcher and pour into 6 wetted 5-oz [150-ml] molds, place on a tray, and leave in the refrigerator until set—at least 4 hours.

4. To serve: Dip the molds briefly into warm water and turn out onto serving plates. Place a small piece of honeycomb on top. Drizzle with a little more honey, pour a little cold cream around the plate, and serve.

Don't be put off by the poppy seeds in this recipe; they add an agreeable crunch. This quick and easy cake is based on the lemon and cornflake cakes we used to make as children—see right.

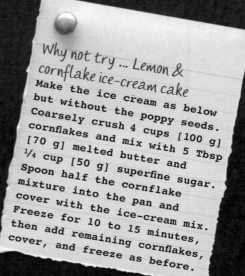

Why not try ... Lemon & cornflake ice-cream cake

Make the ice cream as below but without the poppy seeds. Coarsely crush 4 cups [100 g] cornflakes and mix with 5 Tbsp [70 g] melted butter and ¼ cup [50 g] superfine sugar. Spoon half the cornflake mixture into the pan and cover with the ice-cream mix. Freeze for 10 to 15 minutes, then add remaining cornflakes, cover, and freeze as before.

Poppy seed & lemon ice-cream cake with stewed black currants

SERVES 6

4 lemons

One 13¾-oz [397-g] can sweetened condensed milk

⅝ cup [150 ml] Greek-style plain yogurt

⅝ cup [150 ml] heavy or whipping cream

⅓ cup [50 g] poppy seeds

FOR THE STEWED BLACK CURRANTS:

3½ cups [400 g] black currants

¾ cup [150 g] superfine sugar

1 Tbsp lemon juice

1 tsp arrowroot

1. Line a 1 lb [450-g] loaf pan with parchment paper.

2. Finely grate the zest from 2 of the lemons then squeeze the juice from all 4. Pour the condensed milk into a mixing bowl and gradually beat in the lemon juice and zest. The mixture will naturally thicken. Stir in the yogurt.

3. Lightly whip the cream in a separate bowl into soft peaks and gently fold into the mixture. Stir in the poppy seeds. Pour the mixture into the prepared pan, cover with plastic wrap, and freeze for at least 6 to 8 hours (ideally overnight) until very firm.

4. Meanwhile, put the black currants into a pan with the sugar and lemon juice and pop over low heat. Cook for about 4 minutes, until the sugar has dissolved and the currants are only just starting to burst. Mix the arrowroot with 1 Tbsp cold water, stir in, and simmer for 1 minute until thickened. Tip into a bowl, cool, and then chill until needed.

5. To serve: Remove the ice cream from the freezer and dip the pan briefly in warm water so that you can lift it out. Let it soften slightly for a few minutes, then peel back the paper and cut across into ¼-in [6 to 7 mm] thick slices. Serve with the stewed black currants.

This recipe really is worth a go—it's so much lighter than a traditional bread pudding. Plus you'll be left with half a jar of lemon curd ... a brilliant thing to have up your sleeve.

Lemon curd & raisin bread & butter pudding

SERVES 6

½ cup [100 g] raisins

Finely grated zest of 1 small lemon, plus 1 Tbsp juice

1 small, fresh, pan-shaped loaf of white bread

3½ Tbsp [50 g] soft butter

4 Tbsp homemade or good lemon curd

1 cup [250 ml] whole milk

1 cup [250 ml] heavy cream

3 large free-range eggs

2 Tbsp superfine sugar

Powdered sugar, for dusting

1. Let the raisins soak in the lemon juice for at least 1 hour (or overnight if you remember) so they have time to soften and soak up the juice. Preheat the oven to 375°F [190°C]. Cut seven ¼-in [5-mm] thick slices of bread from the loaf, stack them up, and cut off the crusts. Spread them generously with the butter and lemon curd, then cut each one into 4 triangles.

2. Lay half of the triangles over the bottom of a 1.3-qt [1.5-L] shallow ovenproof dish. Sprinkle over half the raisins, then overlap the rest of the triangles on top, butter-side up. Scatter over the remaining raisins.

3. Mix the milk, cream, eggs, sugar, and lemon zest together, then pour over the top of the bread and let soak for 5 minutes, pushing the top layer of bread down into the liquid now and then.

4. Put the dish into a roasting pan and pour some just-boiled water into the pan to come halfway up the sides of the dish. Bake for 30 minutes until it is puffed up and golden. Remove from the oven and the roasting pan of water. Let rest for a few minutes, dust with powdered sugar and serve warm, with a little extra cream if you fancy.

Or you could try ...

Orange & marmalade bread & butter pudding

Spread the buttered bread with fine-shred marmalade instead of lemon curd and make the custard with the zest of an orange. For a Blueberry & lemon bread & butter pudding, make the pudding as for the main recipe, replacing the lemon-soaked raisins with 1 cup [150 g] fresh blueberries.

When we were children, each week a van would come around the village selling cakes and egg tarts. Mom wasn't too keen, so it was always a challenge to see who could run up and grab one without being spotted.

Deep-filled nutmeg & custard tart

SERVES 8 TO 10

FOR THE PIE DOUGH:

2 cups [225 g] all-purpose flour, plus extra for dusting

Pinch salt

1/2 tsp fresh grated nutmeg

1/2 cup [65 g] powdered sugar

1/2 cup [125 g] chilled butter, cut into small pieces

1 extra-large free-range egg yolk

FOR THE FILLING:

2 1/2 cups [600 ml] heavy cream

1 1/4 cups [300 ml] whole milk

1 large vanilla bean, slit open lengthwise

1/2 cup [100 g] superfine sugar

3 extra-large free-range eggs, plus 3 large yolks

1 1/4 tsp freshly grated nutmeg

1. For the pie dough: Sift the flour, salt, grated nutmeg, and powdered sugar into a food processor. Add the butter and whiz briefly until the mixture looks like fine bread crumbs. Beat the egg yolk briefly with 4 tsp cold water, add to the machine, and whiz until the whole thing comes together into a ball. Turn out onto a lightly floured counter and knead briefly until smooth. Wrap in plastic wrap and chill for 15 minutes, then remove from the refrigerator and thinly roll out. Use to line a 9 1/2-in [24-cm] loose-bottomed tart pan, 2 in [5 cm] deep. Chill for 20 minutes.

2. Preheat the oven to 400°F [200°C]. Line the pastry shell with foil and pie weights and bake on a shelf in the center of the oven for 15 minutes. Remove the foil and weights and bake for another 5 to 7 minutes or until the bottom is crisp and golden brown. Remove and set to aside. Reduce the oven temperature to 300°F [150°C].

3. For the filling: Put the cream, milk, vanilla bean, and sugar into a pan and leave over medium heat until just starting to bubble. Set aside and let infuse for 10 minutes. Meanwhile, put the eggs and egg yolks into a bowl and beat together gently.

4. Pour the hot milk over the beaten eggs, discarding the vanilla bean. Add 1 tsp of the grated nutmeg and mix together well. Strain the mixture through a strainer into a pitcher. Slide out the central oven tray, pop the tart shell onto it, and pour in the filling. Sprinkle over the rest of the nutmeg. Carefully slide it back into the oven and bake for 45 minutes or until the tart is just set and still quite wobbly in the center. Remove from the oven and let cool. Serve warm or cold, cut into wedges.

This delicate, creamy dessert just sings out summer and is great for entertaining. Most of the bits can be prepared in advance and assembled just before serving. Very handy indeed.

Floating islands with red summer berries

SERVES 6

15¾ oz [450 g] mixed red summer berries (red currants, raspberries, and sliced small strawberries)

FOR THE CARAMEL:

¼ cup plus 2 Tbsp [75 g] superfine sugar

1 Tbsp kirsch

FOR THE CUSTARD:

1⅔ cups [400 ml] whole milk

7 Tbsp [100 ml] heavy cream

1 vanilla bean, slit open lengthwise and seeds scraped out

6 extra-large free-range egg yolks

¼ cup [50 g] superfine sugar

2 Tbsp kirsch

FOR THE SOFT MERINGUES:

2 extra-large free-range egg whites

¼ cup [50 g] superfine sugar

1. For the caramel: Warm the sugar and 2 Tbsp water in a small pan over low heat until the sugar has dissolved and the syrup is clear. Turn up the heat and boil until it goes a deep amber-color, then whip off the heat and plunge the pan's bottom into cold water. Carefully add the kirsch and another 2 Tbsp water. Return to low heat and stir until all the caramel bits have dissolved, then let cool. Pour into a pitcher, cover, and set aside until needed.

2. For the custard: Put the milk, cream, vanilla seeds, and bean into a pan, bring to a boil then set aside for 10 minutes. Fish out the bean. Whisk the egg yolks and sugar together in a bowl until pale and creamy, return the milk mixture to a boil, and gradually whisk it into the egg yolks. Pour the lot back into the pan and cook over low heat, stirring constantly, until the mixture thickens and coats the back of a wooden spoon. Strain into a clean bowl and stir in the kirsch. Let cool, then cover and chill for at least 4 hours or until needed.

3. Shortly before serving, make the meringues. Bring 2 cups [500 ml] water to a very gentle simmer in a large frying pan. Whisk the egg whites in a clean bowl until white and foamy, add half the sugar, and whisk into soft peaks. Gradually whisk in the remaining sugar to form a stiff and glossy meringue. Scoop out a large spoonful of the meringue and gently ease it onto the surface of the water. Form 2 more "islands" and let them poach for 3 minutes. Lift out with a slotted spoon onto a rimmed baking sheet lined with a clean dish towel and repeat to make another 3 "islands."

4. To serve: Pour the custard into the bottom of 6 glass dishes or bowls. Float one of the meringue islands on top. Scatter some of the berries around each island and drizzle over a little of the caramel to finish.

This is one of the most popular treats at our tea rooms. We make it with summer fruits as they appear. All you need on the side is a good strong cup of tea.

Raspberry, lemon & yogurt tea loaf

MAKES ONE 2-LB [1-KG] LOAF

2 cups [250 g] all-purpose flour

2 tsp baking powder

Pinch salt

½ cup [115 g] soft butter

Generous 1 cup [225 g] superfine sugar

Finely grated zest and juice of 1 large lemon

2 extra-large free-range eggs

7 Tbsp [100 ml] whole plain yogurt

¼ cup [25 g] ground almonds

1⅔ cups [200 g] fresh raspberries

½ cup [100 g] granulated sugar, plus extra for sprinkling

1. Preheat the oven to 350°F [180°C]. Grease and line a 2-lb [900-g] loaf pan with nonstick parchment paper.

2. Sift together the flour, baking powder, and salt. Cream together the butter and superfine sugar in a large mixing bowl for 5 minutes until pale and fluffy, then beat in the lemon zest. Beat in the eggs, one at a time, adding 1 Tbsp of the sifted flour with the second egg. Alternately fold in large spoonfuls of the remaining flour and the yogurt until the mixture is smooth, then fold in the ground almonds.

3. Spoon a third of the cake batter into the bottom of the loaf pan and scatter over a third of the raspberries. Repeat twice more, ending with a layer of raspberries. Bake for 45 to 50 minutes until the cake is nicely browned, then cover loosely with foil and bake for another 20 to 25 minutes, until a skewer inserted into the middle of the cake comes away clean.

4. Remove the cake from the oven and let cool for 5 minutes. Mix the granulated sugar with the lemon juice, spoon it over the top of the cake, and let soak for 5 minutes. Carefully remove the cake from the pan and pop it on a wire rack to cool.

5. Peel the paper away from the cake and sprinkle the top lightly with a little more sugar. Serve cut into thick slices.

Why not try ...?

Making this cake with fresh blackberries or blueberries instead of raspberries.

the farmhouse kitchen

Ah, baking ... surely the most generous of kitchen activities. Most people don't really bake for themselves but for others, and we're the same. Yes, we love the smells and anticipation of a homemade cake. And the licking of the bowl. But more than that, for us, baking is about sharing the love, both with family and friends. Might sound a bit soppy but it's true.

We're not scientists, but we reckon there's a pretty clear link between baking talent and popularity. Just something we've noticed.

Out of all the different types of cooking, baking has to be the best one to get the children involved in.

What could be better on a Sunday afternoon than raiding the pantry for flour and eggs and making a good old mess?

And then there's the suspense as it's baking in the oven. Will it rise? Will it be moist and delicious? Hopefully with the following recipes the answer is "yes!"

Choc chip cookies

1. Sift 1⅛ cups [225 g] all-purpose flour, ½ tsp baking powder, and ½ tsp salt. Mix ⅔ cup [60 g] unsweetened cocoa together with 7 Tbsp [100 g] melted butter in a bowl until very smooth. Stir in 2¼ cups [450 g] superfine sugar, 1 tsp vanilla extract, and ¼ cup [160 ml] buttermilk. Gradually stir in the flour mixture and scant 1 cup [150 g] chocolate chips.

2. Drop heaping tsp of the dough onto 2 lined baking sheets, leaving 2 in [5 cm] between each one. Bake in a preheated oven at 350°F [180°C] for 7 to 9 minutes, until set and colored. Cool for 2 to 3 minutes, then transfer to a wire rack and cool completely.

Crunchy apple & raspberry granola

MAKES APPROX. 10 SERVINGS

1½ cups [125 g] jumbo oats

1½ cups [125 g] rolled oats

¼ cup [35 g] each blanched whole almonds, skinned hazelnuts, and walnut pieces

2 Tbsp sesame seeds

¼ cup [25 g] sunflower seeds

¼ cup [25 g] pumpkin seeds

3½ Tbsp [50 ml] canola oil

2 Tbsp honey

¼ cup [50 g] light brown sugar

2 Tbsp light tahini paste

³⁄₈ cup [25 g] shredded coconut

1¾ oz [50 g] dried apples or pears, chopped into small pieces

¼ cup [25 g] each dried cranberries, blueberries, and sour cherries

½ oz [15 g] freeze-dried raspberries

1. Preheat the oven to 340°F [170°C]. Pop the oats, nuts, and seeds in a bowl and mix together well. Warm the oil, honey, sugar, and tahini paste together in a small pan until smooth and runny, add to the dry ingredients, and mix well, then scrunch the whole lot together a little with your hands to encourage the mixture to stick together in small clumps.

2. Spread the mixture evenly over a large baking sheet lined with wax paper and bake for 20 minutes, lifting and turning the mixture over after 10 minutes, then every 5 minutes or so after that, taking care not to break up the lumps. Scatter over the flaked coconut and bake for another 5 minutes, by which time everything should be lightly golden. Remove from the oven and let cool. Mix together the dried fruits.

3. Store both mixes separately in airtight containers until needed (they will keep for about a month). Stir them together before serving and serve with lashings of yogurt and/or seasonal fruit compotes.

Apple & honey bircher muesli with fruit & nuts

SERVES 6

2¾ cups [225 g] rolled oats

⁷⁄₈ cup [200 ml] apple juice

1 cup [225 g] whole plain yogurt

2 Tbsp honey

Grated zest of 1 small lemon

2 dessert apples, quartered, cored, and coarsely grated

A CHOICE OF TOPPINGS:

7¾ oz [225 g] chopped apples & ¹⁄₃ cup [50 g] toasted walnuts

1½ cups [225 g] blueberries & ¹⁄₃ cup [50 g] toasted hazelnuts, chopped

1¾ cups [225 g] raspberries & ¹⁄₃ cup [50 g] toasted pecans

7¾ oz [225 g] chopped pears & ¹⁄₃ cup [50 g] toasted almonds, chopped

1. Mix the oats, ⁷⁄₈ cup [200 ml] cold water, and the apple juice together in a bowl. Cover with plastic wrap and chill overnight.

2. The next morning, stir in the yogurt, honey, lemon zest, and grated apples. Spoon into individual bowls and sprinkle with the topping of your choice.

Our children love making these pancakes; well, they're so simple to cook. Feel free to sprinkle some fresh fruit over them while they're frying. Raspberries and strawberries work well, as do slices of banana.

Buttermilk pancakes with honey & vanilla butter

SERVES 4

3/4 cup [100 g] self-rising flour

1 tsp baking powder

2 Tbsp superfine sugar

Pinch salt

2 extra-large free-range eggs, separated

3/4 cup [175 ml] buttermilk

3 Tbsp whole milk

3 Tbsp [45 g] butter, melted and cooled

FOR THE HONEY & VANILLA BUTTER:

7 Tbsp [100 g] soft butter

3 Tbsp honey

1 tsp vanilla bean paste

1. For the butter: Simply beat the ingredients together with an electric whisk until pale and creamy. Spoon into a small bowl and let firm slightly in the refrigerator for 1 hour.

2. For the pancakes: Sift the flour, baking powder, sugar, and salt into a bowl. Make a well in the middle and add the egg yolks, buttermilk, milk, and 1 Tbsp of the melted butter. Whisk together to make a smooth batter. Pop the egg whites into a large clean bowl and whisk into soft peaks, then gently fold into the batter.

3. Heat a large nonstick frying pan over medium heat. Brush the bottom with a little of the melted butter. Add 3 to 4 large spoonfuls of the batter, spaced well apart, to the pan and cook for 2 minutes until bubbles start to appear in the top of the mixture, and they are golden brown underneath. Turn over and cook for 1 minute more. Serve in batches as you cook them or put them onto a plate, cover with a clean dish towel, and keep warm in a low oven while you cook the remainder. Serve hot with the honey and vanilla butter.

Or you could try ...

Ricotta pancakes. Replace half the buttermilk with 3/4 cup [175 g] ricotta cheese. Serve with sliced raw or pan-fried bananas and the vanilla and honey butter.

Bacon & maple syrup pancakes. In Holland they love to serve pancakes with maple syrup and crispy bacon. If you haven't already tried it, give it a go—it's a great combination of salty and sweet.

Farls are very similar to soda bread, but the mixture is cut into wedges before cooking. This recipe will make eight farls, so serve one or two per person. Hungry farmers tend to polish off two each with no problem.

Cheddar farls with fried eggs & crispy bacon

SERVES 4

FOR THE FARLS:

3³/₄ cups [450 g] self-rising flour, plus extra for kneading

1 tsp baking soda

1 tsp English mustard powder

2 tsp yellow mustard seeds, lightly crushed

1¹/₃ cups [150 g] finely grated cheddar

Scant 1¹/₄ cups [280 ml] buttermilk, mixed with 6 Tbsp [90 ml] whole milk

Salt and freshly ground black pepper

TO SERVE:

4 strings of cherry tomatoes on the vine

A little olive oil

12 slices dry-cured lean bacon, smoked or unsmoked

4 extra-large free-range eggs

Sunflower oil, for shallow-frying

Butter, for spreading

1. Preheat the oven to 425°F [220°C]. Sift the flour, baking soda, 1 tsp salt, and mustard powder together into a bowl and stir in the mustard seeds and cheddar. Make a well in the center, add the buttermilk mixture, and mix together into a soft, slightly sticky dough.

2. Turn the dough out onto a lightly floured counter and quickly and gently shape it into a 8¹/₂-in [22-cm] circle. Lift it onto a lightly floured nonstick baking sheet and cut into 8 wedges. Separate the wedges to give them room to rise and spread, sprinkle with a bit more flour, and bake for 20 minutes until golden brown.

3. While the farls are cooking, put the strings of cherry tomatoes into a small roasting pan, drizzle with a little olive oil, and season lightly. After the farls have been cooking for 10 minutes, slide the pan of tomatoes alongside and roast for 10 minutes.

4. Meanwhile, pop a grill pan over high heat until smoking, reduce the heat to medium, and cook the bacon until crisp and golden. At the same time, shallow-fry the eggs until done to your liking. (We like ours with the edges crispy but the yolks still runny.)

5. Remove the farls from the oven, slice them in half, and spread with butter. Fill with the bacon slices, top with the eggs, and serve with the tomatoes.

Or how about ...?

Scallion & yogurt farls. Add 8 to 10 sliced scallions to the dry mixture and use ¹/₂ cup [140 g] yogurt mixed with ¹/₂ cup [140 ml] milk instead of the buttermilk.

OK, major top tip coming up. If you want to make the lightest scones ever, we have a secret ingredient for you: yogurt. Something to do with the way it reacts with the baking powder. These beauties always go down a storm at our tea room.

White chocolate, yogurt & sour cherry scones

MAKES 12 SCONES

3³/₄ cups [450 g] self-rising flour

large pinch salt

4 tsp baking powder

7 Tbsp [100 g] chilled butter, diced

¹/₄ cup [50 g] superfine sugar

1²/₃ cups [150 g] dried sour cherries, halved

³/₄ cup [150 g] white chocolate chunks or chips for cooking

2 large free-range eggs

7 Tbsp [100 ml] whole plain yogurt

approx. ⁷/₈ cup [200 ml] whole milk

granulated sugar, for sprinkling

1. Preheat the oven to 425°F [220°C]. Sift the flour, salt, and baking powder into the bowl of a food processor, add the butter, and whiz until the mixture looks like fine bread crumbs. Tip into a bowl and stir in the superfine sugar, cherries, and chocolate.

2. Put the eggs and yogurt into a measuring cup and make up to 1³/₄ cups [400 ml] with the milk. Make a well in the center of the dried ingredients, add all but 2 Tbsp of the milky mixture and very lightly mix to make a soft, slightly sticky dough. Don't overmix!

3. Turn the dough out onto a lightly floured counter and knead lightly and briefly, until just smooth. Lightly pat out the dough until it is about 1¹/₄ in [3 cm] thick. Cut out as many scones as you can using a floured 2³/₄-in [7-cm] cutter. Gently reknead and pat out the trimmings twice more to make 12 scones.

4. Place the scones, slightly apart, on a large greased baking sheet and brush with the remaining milky mixture. Sprinkle with a little granulated sugar and bake for 12 to 15 minutes until puffed up, golden brown, and cooked through.

5. Lift onto a wire rack and let cool, then eat as soon as possible with lashings of butter and jam.

Or you could try ...
Cranberry & orange scones. Use 1¹/₄ cups [150 g] dried cranberries mixed with 3¹/₂ oz [100 g] chopped candied orange instead of the chocolate/cherries and add the grated zest of an orange to the egg mix.

This is a lovely, moist cake, partly thanks to yesterday's newspaper. Tying a thick band around the pan before it goes in the oven helps stop the outside cooking too quickly and drying out.

Cider & apple cake

MAKES ONE 9-IN [23-CM] CAKE

1³/₄ cups [215 g] all-purpose flour

1³/₄ Tbsp cornstarch

1½ tsp baking powder

½ tsp salt

¼ tsp ground cinnamon

¼ tsp ground cloves

¼ tsp ground ginger

¼ tsp freshly grated nutmeg

1½ cups [300 g] superfine sugar, plus extra for sprinkling

³/₄ cup [175 g] soft unsalted butter

2 large free-range eggs

3 Tbsp hard cider

15³/₄ oz [450 g] peeled and cored dessert apples, cut into ½-in [1-cm] pieces

½ cup [75 g] raisins

1 cup [100 g] lightly toasted walnuts, broken into small pieces

1. Preheat the oven to 350°F [180°C]. Grease and line a 9-in [23-cm] round, loose-bottomed cake pan with nonstick paper. Tie a thick band of folded newspaper around the outside of the pan and secure with string.

2. Sift the flour, cornstarch, baking powder, salt, and spices into the bowl of a stand mixer. Add the sugar and butter and beat together on a medium speed for 1 minute until well mixed.

3. Add the eggs and mix on low speed for a few seconds, then increase the speed and beat for 1 minute until light and fluffy. Beat in the cider.

4. Fold in the prepared apples, raisins, and walnuts. The mixture will look very thick, but don't worry. Spoon it into the prepared pan and level the surface.

5. Bake for about 1¼ hours, covering the cake loosely with foil once it is richly browned on top, until firm to the touch, and a skewer inserted into the center of it comes away clean. Let cool in the pan on a wire rack, then remove from the pan to a plate, sprinkle with superfine sugar, and serve.

Or how about ...?

Pear, pecan, and date cake. Use firm, ripe pears instead of the apples, pecans instead of the walnuts, and chopped soft dried dates instead of the raisins. This cake is also lovely made with brown sugar instead of superfine sugar.

When we were little, we'd run out to the fields with thick slices of this cake for all the people making hay. We still remember the joy on their faces as they munched away, sitting on top of the bales.

Farmhouse fruit cake

MAKES ONE 9-IN [23 CM] CAKE

1¼ lb [550 g] mixed dried fruit (we like raisins, cranberries, blueberries, sour cherries, and chopped candied peel)

3¾ cups [450 g] self-rising flour

1½ tsp mixed spice

Large pinch salt

1¼ cups [300 g] soft butter

1½ cups [300 g] superfine sugar

4 large free-range eggs

¾ cup [200 ml] whole milk

2 Tbsp raw brown sugar

1. Put the mixed dried fruit into a bowl with ½ cup [120 ml] hot water. Stir together well and let soak for 1 hour, stirring now and then. Meanwhile, grease and line a 9-in [23-cm] deep, round, loose-bottomed cake pan with nonstick parchment paper. Make a deep band from a few folded sheets of newspaper and tie it around the outside of the pan.

2. Preheat the oven to 300°F [150°C]. Spread the soaked dried fruits out onto a clean dish towel and dry well. Tip into a bowl, toss with 2 Tbsp of the flour, and set aside. Sift the remaining flour into a separate bowl with the mixed spice and salt.

3. Cream the butter and superfine sugar together for 5 minutes until pale and fluffy. Beat in the eggs, one at a time, adding 1 Tbsp of the sifted flour with the last 2 eggs. Fold in the rest of the flour in 2 batches, alternating with the milk, until smooth, then fold in the dried fruits.

4. Spoon the batter into the pan and lightly level the top, then sprinkle over the raw brown sugar. Bake the cake in the center of the oven for about 1¾ hours, until a skewer inserted into the cake comes away clean, and it has just started to show signs of shrinking away from the sides of the pan. Let the cake cool in the pan for 5 minutes, then remove and let cool on a wire rack.

If you've never tried a blondie, all we can say is you really must. They're like brownies but, well, blonde. That'll be the white chocolate! These ones are also wonderful served warm with ice cream.

Or how about ...?
Dark chocolate and raspberry brownies

Melt 1 cup [250 g] butter with 9 oz [250 g] semisweet chocolate. Whisk the eggs, sugar, and vanilla as before and fold in the chocolate, flour, ½ cup [50 g] ground almonds, and 1 cup [100 g] raspberries. Pour the batter into the pan, scatter 1 cup [100 g] raspberries on top, and bake for 30 to 35 minutes.

Red currant & white chocolate blondies

MAKES 16

8¾ oz [250 g] good white chocolate

½ cup [125 g] butter

4 extra-large free-range eggs

1¾ cups [350 g] superfine sugar

2 tsp vanilla extract

1¼ cups [150 g] all-purpose flour

½ tsp salt

1⅔ cups [150 g] ground almonds

1¾ cups [200 g] fresh red currants, stripped from their stalks

Powdered sugar, for dusting (optional)

1. Grease and line a rectangular 8-by-12-in [20-by-30-cm] cake pan or brownie pan with nonstick parchment paper. Preheat the oven to 340°F [170°C].

2. Put the white chocolate and butter into a heatproof bowl, sit it over a pan of barely simmering water, and melt very gently, stirring regularly until smooth. (Take care not to let it get too hot or it will "seize" and go grainy.) Set aside to cool slightly.

3. Beat the eggs, sugar, and vanilla extract together, in a stand mixer or by hand, for 10 minutes until really thick and moussy. Gently fold in the melted chocolate, then sift over and fold in the flour and salt. Fold in the ground almonds and red currants.

4. Pour the batter into the prepared pan and bake for 35 to 40 minutes, until firm and shiny on top and a skewer pushed into the center of the cake comes away with some very sticky crumbs clinging to it.

5. Let cool in the pan for 10 minutes or so, then carefully lift it onto a wire rack and let cool until cold. Cut into squares and dust with powdered sugar if you wish.

Honeycomb might seem rather an odd thing to make yourself but it's actually really easy, and good fun. The way it fizzes up when you add the baking soda—wonderful!

Honeycomb & chocolate cookie cake

MAKES APPROX. 24 PIECES

½ cup [115 ml] heavy cream

1¼ lb [600 g] good semisweet chocolate (70% cocoa solids), broken into pieces

¾ cup [165 g] butter

1 cup [100 g] dried sour cherries, blueberries, or raisins

2¾ oz [75 g] (approx. 9) Savoiardi cookies, cut into 1-in [2.5-cm] pieces

Unsweetened cocoa, for dusting

FOR THE HONEYCOMB:

2½ cups [500 g] superfine sugar

⅓ cup [125 g] liquid glucose

¼ cup [100 g] honey

1 Tbsp baking soda, loaded into a tea strainer ready for sifting

1. For the honeycomb: Oil and line an 8-by-12-in [20-by-30-cm] loaf pan with parchment paper, making sure the paper comes at least 2 in [5 cm] above the edges. Put the sugar, glucose, honey, and 6 Tbsp [90 ml] water in a pan over low heat and stir until the sugar has dissolved and the syrup is clear. Bring to a boil, put a sugar thermometer into the pan, and boil rapidly without stirring until it reaches 302°F [150°C].

2. When the sugar syrup reaches the right temperature, turn off the heat, quickly sift over the baking soda, and whisk in vigorously. The mixture will froth up, become lighter, and start rising up the sides of the pan. As it reaches the top, pour it into the pan. Leave it for 30 minutes to go cold and become brittle.

3. Lightly oil and line a 8-in [20-cm] square shallow pan with nonstick parchment paper. Put ⅓ cup [85 ml] of the cream, 15¾ oz [450 g] of the chocolate, and ½ cup [125 g] of the butter into a medium pan and the remaining cream, chocolate, and butter into another smaller pan. Stir the larger pan of mixture over low heat until it has melted.

4. Put 5¼ oz [150 g] of the honeycomb in a plastic bag and break into raisin-size pieces with a rolling pin. Put into a bowl with the fruit and cookies, then pour over the melted chocolate mixture and stir together. Scoop it into the pan, spread it out to the edges, and level the top.

5. Gently melt the remaining chocolate mixture, pour it into the pan, and spread out to fill out any gaps. Chill for 3 hours or until set. Remove from the pan, cut lengthwise in half, and across into fingers, dust with cocoa, and let soften slightly before serving.

These delicious fingers are kind of like posh bakewell tarts. They're a great way to use up any leftover jam you might have lurking in the back of your pantry.

Blackberry & brown sugar fingers

MAKES 16 FINGERS

FOR THE BASE:

Scant 1 cup [225 g] soft butter

½ cup plus 2 Tbsp [75 g] sifted powdered sugar

Scant 2 cups [225 g] all-purpose flour

Scant ½ cup [50 g] cornstarch

Pinch salt

½ cup [200 g] blackberry jam

FOR THE TOPPING:

½ cup [125 g] soft butter

½ cup plus 2 Tbsp [125 g] packed light brown sugar

Finely grated zest of 1 lemon

2 extra-large free-range eggs, beaten

2 Tbsp self-rising flour

2 cups [175 g] ground almonds

1⅓ cups [200 g] blackberries

¼ cup [25 g] slivered almonds

1 Tbsp raw brown sugar, plus extra for sprinkling

1. Preheat the oven to 350°F [180°C]. Grease and line an 8 by 12-in [20 by 30-cm] loose-bottomed brownie pan with nonstick parchment paper.

2. For the base: Cream the butter and powdered sugar together in a bowl until pale and fluffy. Sift over the flour, cornstarch, and salt and stir into the butter mixture to make a soft, shortbreadlike dough. Roll the dough out on a lightly floured counter almost to the size of the pan, lower into the pan, and press out a little to the edges. Prick here and there with a fork and bake for 16 minutes until a pale cookie color. Remove and let cool until cold, then spread with the jam to within ½ in [1 cm] of the edges.

3. For the topping: Cream the butter and brown sugar together until light and fluffy. Beat in the lemon zest. Gradually beat in the beaten eggs, then fold in the flour and ground almonds. Dollop small spoonfuls of mixture over the jam and carefully spread it out in an even layer. Scatter over the blackberries, pushing half of them down into the mix.

4. Sprinkle over the Tbsp of raw brown sugar and bake for 10 minutes. Carefully slide out the oven shelf, sprinkle over the slivered almonds, and bake for another 30 minutes, or until golden brown and a skewer pushed into the topping comes out clean. Remove, sprinkle with a little more raw brown sugar, and let cool in the pan. Then cut lengthwise in half, and across into 16 fingers.

Ginger cake and parkin are two of our favorite wintertime treats. This easy-to-make recipe is made extra moreish by virtue of some rather special fudgelike frosting.

Ginger cake with fudgy frosting

MAKES ONE 9-IN [23-CM]
SQUARE CAKE

scant 1 cup [225 g] butter

1 1/8 cups [225 g] packed
dark brown sugar

1/2 cup [200 g] light corn syrup

1 Tbsp blackstrap molasses

2 extra-large free-range
eggs, beaten

1 1/4 cups [300 ml] whole milk

3 1/8 cups [375 g] all-purpose
flour

large pinch salt

2 tsp baking soda

2 tsp ground ginger

FOR THE FUDGY FROSTING:

5 Tbsp [75 g] butter

3/4 cup [180 ml] heavy cream

1/4 cup plus 2 Tbsp [75 g]
superfine sugar

1/4 cup plus 2 Tbsp [75 g]
packed light brown sugar

pinch salt

1. Preheat the oven to 300°F [150°C]. Grease and line a 9-in [23-cm] square cake pan with nonstick parchment paper.

2. Put the butter, sugar, syrup, and molasses into a pan and stir over low heat until melted. Let cool slightly, then stir in the eggs and milk.

3. Sift the flour, salt, baking soda, and ground ginger into a mixing bowl and make a well in the center. Add the liquid mixture and beat together until smooth.

4. Pour the batter into the pan and bake for about 1 hour or until well risen and firm to the touch. Let cool in the pan for 10 minutes, then turn out and let cool until cold on a wire rack.

5. For the frosting: Put the ingredients into a pan and stir over medium heat until melted. Bring to a boil and simmer for 5 minutes, stirring now and then. Remove from the heat and beat with a wooden spoon until the mixture has thickened to a toffee saucelike consistency. Cool completely, beating occasionally to prevent it forming a sugary skin. When cold beat vigorously, until thick and spreadable.

6. Spoon the frosting onto the top of the cake and spread out in an even layer, then swirl with the blade of the knife. Let set completely before cutting into slices to serve.

MAKES 2 SMALL LOAVES

3⅓ cups [400 g] stoneground wholewheat flour

1⅔ cups [200 g] all-purpose white flour, plus a little extra for flouring

1 rounded tsp baking soda

1 tsp salt

Approx. 2½ cups [600 ml] buttermilk

Living on a farm and making bread seem to go hand in hand. Don't panic if the dough seems sticky, this is how it should be. Avoid adding extra flour: hold your nerve, knead gently, and you'll be rewarded with a delightfully moist loaf.

Stoneground soda bread

1. Preheat the oven to 450°F [230°C].

2. Mix the flours, baking soda, and salt together in a large mixing bowl. Make a well in the center, pour in most of the buttermilk, and mix together, adding a little more buttermilk if necessary, until it comes together into a soft, sticky dough.

3. Turn the dough out onto a lightly floured counter and knead very lightly and briefly until it comes together into a ball. Cut the dough in half and knead each piece briefly once more into a smooth circle. Do not overknead the mixture, as this will make the bread very heavy. Slightly flatten each circle into 1½-in [4-cm] thick disks. Place them well apart on a baking sheet lightly dusted with flour, then, using a large, sharp knife, cut a large, deep cross into the top of each loaf, to within about ½ in [1 cm] of the bottom.

4. Bake the loaves on the middle shelf of the oven for 15 minutes, then lower the oven temperature to 400°F [200°C] and bake for another 10 minutes, until they are well risen and have developed a rich, golden brown crust. They should sound hollow when you tap their bases. Cool on a wire rack. Eat on the same day as baking.

Or you could try ...

Cheesy oat bread. Replace 2 Tbsp of the wholewheat flour with rolled oats and stir ⅔ cup [75 g] grated cheddar into the dry flour mixture. Before you cut the cross into the top of the loaf, sprinkle it with another scant ½ cup [50 g] grated cheese and a few more oats. **Rosemary & olive bread.** Add 2 Tbsp chopped rosemary and ½ cup [100 g] coarsely chopped pitted green olives to the dry flour mixture. **Sundried tomato & thyme bread.** Add scant 2 cups [100 g] coarsely chopped sundried tomatoes and 2 Tbsp picked thyme leaves to the dry flour mixture.

This is an unusual but wonderful bread,
which we make with our homemade cider.
Studded with lovely dried fruits and nuts,
it goes really well with soup or some good cheese.

Cider, honey, walnut & raisin bread

MAKES 2 LARGE LOAVES

1 cup [175 g] raisins

4¼ cups [500 g] strong white bread flour, plus extra for flouring

4¼ cups [500 g] stoneground wholewheat flour

3½ tsp [10 g] active dry yeast

3½ tsp salt

2 Tbsp honey

2 cups [500 ml] hard cider

2 cups [200 g] lightly toasted walnut pieces

1. Cover the raisins with 3½ Tbsp boiling water and soak overnight. Drain and pat dry with paper towels.

2. Put the flours, yeast, and salt into a large mixing bowl or the bowl of a stand mixer. Warm the honey, cider, and ⅞ cup [200 ml] water in a small pan, add to the bowl, and mix everything together into a dough. Knead the dough for 10 minutes until smooth and elastic, then pop it in a lightly oiled bowl, cover tightly with oiled plastic wrap and a dish towel, and let rise somewhere warm for 1 to 2 hours until doubled in size.

3. Turn the dough out onto a lightly floured counter or into the bowl of the stand mixer and knead for 2 to 3 minutes, then knead in the raisins and walnuts. Divide the dough in half and knead each piece into a neat circle, then put each loaf onto a well-floured baking sheet. Cover again with oiled plastic wrap and a dish towel and let rise once more until doubled in size.

4. Preheat the oven to its highest temperature. 5 minutes before baking, put a small roasting tray of boiling hot water into the bottom of the oven.

5. Put the loaves onto the middle shelf of the oven and bake for 10 minutes. Lower the oven temperature to 350°F [180°C] and bake for another 20 minutes until they are nicely browned and sound hollow when tapped on the base. Let cool on a wire rack.

Or you could try ...
Quick rye bread. Replace the wholewheat flour with rye flour. Use 4 Tbsp caraway seeds instead of the honey, raisins, and walnuts, and use water for the dough.

Oh, how we love the quince. Unspeakably hard and tart when raw, but when cooked: sweet, sumptuous, and fragrant. It's also the fruit that gave marmalade its name—"marmelo" being Portuguese for "quince."

Quince & orange marmalade

MAKES APPROX. SIX 14-OZ [400-G] JARS

15¾ oz [450 g] ordinary oranges (not Seville)

3 lb [1.35 kg] ripe quinces, peeled and cored

6¾ cups [1.35 kg] granulated sugar

1. Pare the zest from the oranges with a sharp potato peeler, leaving behind as much of the white pith as you can. Cut each strip lengthwise into fine shreds. Halve the fruit, squeeze out the juice, and set aside.

2. Put the prepared quince into a food processor fitted with the coarse shredding blade and whiz into strips. Put them into a bowl and stir in the orange juice.

3. Sterilize your jars as on page 72 and pop a few saucers in the freezer to chill. Put the zest and 6½ cups [1.5 L] water in a preserving pan or large saucepan and simmer for 20 minutes. Add the quince mixture, return to a boil, and simmer for 5 minutes, until tender.

4. Add the sugar to the pan and stir over low heat until completely dissolved. Bring the mixture to a rapid boil and boil until setting point is reached. (This will take between 20 and 30 minutes, depending on the ripeness of your fruit.) After 15 minutes, draw the pan off the heat, spoon a little of the marmalade onto one of the chilled saucers, and return to the freezer for a few minutes until cold. Push your finger across the surface—if it wrinkles into a peak with no liquid running back it's done. If not, continue to boil, testing at 3 minute intervals.

5. As soon as setting point has been reached, remove the pan from the heat, stir to disperse any scum, and let settle and cool slightly for 20 minutes.

6. Skim any scum from the surface, then ladle into the hot sterilized jars, filling them to within ¼ in [6 mm] of the top. Press a waxed disk onto the marmalade's surface and seal with lids while still hot. Label and store in a cool dark place. It will keep for at least 2 years.

This is one of our favorite flavor combinations: the tang of the rhubarb, the sweetness of the strawberries ... wonderful! The rhubarb also has a practical role— the pectin inside helps the jam to set.

Strawberry & rhubarb jam

MAKES 7 TO 8 X 12¼-OZ [350-g] JARS

2¼ lb [1 kg] young, trimmed rhubarb stalks, wiped clean

2¼ lb [1 kg] small strawberries, washed and hulled

6 Tbsp lemon juice

9 cups [1.8 kg] preserving sugar

1 Tbsp [15 g] unsalted butter

1. Cut the rhubarb into ³/₄-in [2-cm] pieces. Put into a large bowl with the strawberries, lemon juice, and sugar and stir together well. Cover with a dish towel and leave somewhere cool but not in the refrigerator, overnight. This will draw out some of the juices from the fruit and help to keep the strawberries whole during cooking.

2. The next day, put 3 or 4 saucers into the freezer and prepare your jam jars. Preheat the oven to 300°F [150°C]. Wash your jars and lids in hot soapy water, rinse well, and drain briefly. Transfer to the oven and leave for at least 15 minutes before using.

3. Transfer the fruit mixture to a preserving pan or large, deep saucepan (of at least 4 qt/4.5 L capacity) and heat gently, stirring frequently, until the sugar has completely dissolved. Add the butter and bring to a rolling boil.

4. Boil the jam rapidly for 8 to 10 minutes, until it reaches between 219 to 221°F [104 to 105°C], then draw the pan off the heat and check for setting point. Spoon a little jam onto one of the chilled saucers, return it to the freezer, and leave for 2 minutes. Then push your finger through it. If it wrinkles up into a peak with no liquid running back onto the saucer, it's ready. If it doesn't, boil for another 2 to 3 minutes and retest. Remove from the heat, skim off any scum, and let cool for 15 to 20 minutes or until the fruit stays suspended in the jam after you've stirred it. If you pot your jam too early the fruit will just float back to the surface.

5. Ladle the jam into the warm, sterilized jars using a jam funnel, cover immediately with waxed disks and lids, then label and date. It will keep in a cool dry place for up to 6 months.

the veg garden

A few years ago, Sarah Mead, Tim's wife, breathed new life into our organic gardens, transforming them into one of the most beautiful and fascinating parts of the farm. This is where we grow lots of lovely vegetables, everything from fava beans to beet—most of them destined for dishes served at our HQ and tea room.

The snail is James our head gardener's nemesis. He spends a lot of his time devising ingenious ways of putting them off.

They're persistent little pests, mind. A friend of ours once took a load five miles down the road, after marking their shells with pen. Within a few days they were back!

Growing your own vegetables really makes you appreciate the joys of seasonality.

Once you get used to freshly picked asparagus in May, the idea of eating the imported stuff in December just seems a bit crazy.

At the heart of any great garden is great compost, so we only ever make our own.

And because we're organic, rather than using chemical feeds, we make a special type of "tea" out of comfrey, a boragelike herb.

It's brimming with nitrogen, phosphorus, and potassium. All things our veggies love.

The key to this recipe is to use superfresh eggs. That way the whites will stay together beautifully as you poach them. The farmers' market is always a good bet for eggs, as they're normally days rather than weeks old.

Cream of asparagus soup with soft-poached eggs

SERVES 4

1¼ lb [600 g] fine asparagus

4½ cups [1 L] good vegetable or chicken broth

½ tsp white wine vinegar

4 large, really fresh free-range eggs

¼ cup [65 g] unsalted butter

5¼ oz [150 g] leeks, white part only, trimmed and thinly sliced

2 small celery stalks, thinly sliced

2 Tbsp all-purpose flour

1½ Tbsp heavy cream

Salt and freshly ground black pepper

1. Rinse the asparagus, snap off the woody ends, and coarsely chop them. Put the chopped ends in a pan with the stock, bring to a boil, cover, and simmer for 15 minutes. Strain, discarding the ends, and set the stock aside.

2. Meanwhile, cut the tips off the asparagus spears and halve lengthwise. Coarsely chop the remaining stalks. Bring 2 small pans of lightly salted water to a boil. Drop the asparagus tips into one pan and cook for 2 minutes until just tender. Drain, refresh under cold water, and set aside. Add the vinegar to the second pan and lower the heat. Swirl the water with a spoon to make a whirlpool, crack in an egg, and poach for 3 minutes, then carefully remove with a slotted spoon and set aside on paper towels. Repeat with the remaining eggs, leaving the water to simmer.

3. Melt 3½ Tbsp of the butter in a large pan, add the asparagus stalks, sliced leeks, and celery, cover, and cook over low heat for 10 minutes until soft but not browned.

4. Uncover, stir in the flour and cook for another minute. Stir in the asparagus-flavored broth, cover again, and simmer for 10 minutes until the veg are tender. Remove from the heat, cool slightly, then blend the soup in batches until smooth. Pass through a strainer back into a clean pan, bring back to a simmer, and stir in the cream. Season to taste.

5. Melt the remaining butter. Lower the eggs back into the simmering water and leave for 30 seconds. Remove and drain on paper towels. Ladle the soup into warmed bowls and scatter over the asparagus tips. Place a poached egg into each bowl, season to taste, drizzle over the melted butter, and serve.

This is an excellent soup for dealing with a glut of tomatoes, should you be lucky enough to have that problem. It's delicious with some basil pesto or black olive tapenade swirled through just before serving.

Slow-roasted tomato soup with chile & cheese cornmeal muffins

SERVES 6 TO 8

3³/₄ lb [1.75 kg] tomatoes

⁵/₈ cup [150 ml] olive oil, plus extra for garnish

4 large garlic cloves, chopped

The leaves from 3 large thyme sprigs, plus extra to garnish

The leaves from three 7-in [18-cm] rosemary sprigs

3 medium onions, halved and thinly sliced

3 fat celery stalks, sliced

¹/₂ tsp fennel seeds, lightly crushed

¹/₂ tsp crushed dried chiles

5 cups [1.2 L] good vegetable or light chicken broth

1 Tbsp tomato paste

2 tsp superfine sugar

Juice of 1 lime

Salt and freshly ground black pepper

FOR THE MUFFINS:

1 cup [115 g] all-purpose flour

1 Tbsp baking powder

¹/₄ tsp salt

³/₄ cup [100 g] dried cornmeal

³/₄ cup [85 g] finely grated cheddar

¹/₄ tsp crushed dried chiles

1 large free-range egg, beaten

³/₄ cup [175 ml] whole milk

¹/₂ Tbsp [50 g] butter, melted

1. Preheat the oven to 375°F [190°C]. Halve the tomatoes and lay them cut-side up in a single layer in a large, lightly oiled roasting pan. Sprinkle with salt, pepper, and a few Tbsp of oil and roast for 45 minutes to 1 hour, depending on their size, until they have shriveled and concentrated in flavor.

2. Meanwhile, pour the remaining oil into a large pan and add the garlic, thyme, and rosemary. Place over medium heat and as soon as everything is sizzling nicely, add the onions, celery, fennel seeds, and dried chile. Stir well, cover, and cook over low heat for 20 minutes, uncovering and stirring once or twice, until the onion is very soft but not browned.

3. Add 2¹/₂ cups [600 ml] of the broth, bring to a simmer, and cook, covered, for 10 more minutes. Uncover, add the tomatoes and juices from the pan, the tomato paste, and sugar and simmer for 2 to 3 minutes. Remove from the heat, let cool slightly, then blend in batches until smooth. Strain into a clean pan and stir in enough broth to give the soup a good consistency.

4. For the muffins: Increase the oven to 400°F [200°C]. Line a muffin pan with 8 deep nonstick paper liners. Sift the flour, baking powder, and salt into a mixing bowl and stir in the cornmeal, ²/₃ cup [75 g] of the grated cheese, and the dried chiles. Make a well in the center, add the egg, milk, and melted butter and mix everything together, then spoon the batter into the paper liners. Sprinkle with the remaining grated cheese and bake in the oven for 20 minutes until well-risen and golden.

5. Shortly before the muffins are ready, gently reheat the soup. Add the lime juice and season to taste with salt and pepper. Serve with the muffins.

SERVES 8

15¾ oz [450 g] freshly shelled fava beans

⅓ oz [10 g] basil leaves, torn into pieces

Scant ½ cup [50 g] finely grated pecorino romano

2 tbsp extra-virgin olive oil

1 tsp lemon juice

Salt and freshly ground black pepper

TO SERVE:

One 8¾-oz [250-g] buffalo mozzarella (drained weight)

16 small slices of bread

1 large garlic clove, peeled and halved

1 oz [25 g] wild arugula leaves

Lemon-infused extra-virgin olive oil

Sea salt flakes

Fava bean pâté on toast with torn mozzarella, basil, & lemon oil

1. Drop the fava beans into a pan of well-salted boiling water and cook for 2 to 3 minutes until just tender. Drain, run under cold water to cool, then nick the skin of each bean with your fingernail and pop the bright green beans out of their skins.

2. Put the skinned beans and torn basil leaves into the bowl of a food processor and briefly blitz into a coarse paste. Stir in the grated cheese, olive oil, and lemon juice and season to taste.

3. Tear the mozzarella into small chunks and drain on paper towels. Toast the bread slices on both sides and, while they are still warm, rub one cut face lightly with the peeled garlic clove. Spread generously with some of the fava bean pâté and top with the mozzarella pieces. Arrange them on a large serving plate and scatter over the arugula leaves. Drizzle with some of the lemon olive oil, sprinkle with a few sea salt flakes, and serve straightaway.

Spelt is an ancient grain that's a bit like wheat. It seems to have come back into fashion recently, which pleases us greatly. It's wholesome, hearty, and you can now pick it up from decent grocery stores.

Apple, celery, fennel & spelt salad with cranberries & pomegranate molasses dressing

SERVES 6

1¼ cups [125 g] spelt grain or Italian farro

1½ Tbsp extra-virgin olive oil

1 Tbsp pomegranate molasses

¼ tsp sumac, or to taste

½ cup [50 g] walnut halves

A 7-oz [200-g] bulb of fennel, outer leaves removed

2 chunky celery stalks

2 small dessert apples

1½ Tbsp coarsely chopped mint leaves

1½ Tbsp coarsely chopped fennel herb

2 Tbsp coarsely chopped Italian parsley

scant ¼ cup [50 g] dried cranberries

salt and freshly ground black pepper

1. Preheat the oven to 400°F [200°C]. Rinse the spelt well, drain, and pop into a pan with 3 cups [750 ml] cold water. Bring to a boil, cover, and simmer for 45 minutes, or until tender but still with a little bit of a bite. Drain well, tip into a bowl, and stir in the oil, pomegranate molasses, sumac, ¼ tsp salt, and some black pepper. Let cool.

2. Spread the walnuts on a baking sheet and roast for 6 minutes. Let cool, then break into small pieces.

3. Cut the fennel heart in half and slice widthwise very finely with a sharp knife or on a mandolin. Thinly slice the celery. Quarter and core the apples and cut them into ½-in [1-cm] pieces.

4. Stir the chopped herbs into the spelt followed by the fennel, celery, apples, walnuts, and cranberries. Season to taste and serve straightaway.

Top tip:

If you can't get hold of pomegranate molasses or sumac, use a little honey and some freshly squeezed lemon juice in their place.

Choose pears that are ripe but still have a bit of crunch. Those with a pink-yellow blush to them will look lovely in this salad. And the caramelized walnuts are to die for!

Fall salad with pears, pomegranate seeds, blue cheese & caramelized walnuts

SERVES 4 TO 6

2 ripe but firm dessert pears

1 Tbsp lemon juice

2 small heads green endive, broken into separate leaves

2 small heads red endive, broken into separate leaves

1½ oz [40 g] watercress sprigs

1¾ oz [50 g] radicchio leaves (optional)

3½ oz [100 g] derinded blue cheese, such as Devon Blue, Beenleigh Blue, or Colston Bassett, thinly sliced

The seeds from ½ pomegranate

FOR THE CARAMELIZED WALNUTS:

1 cup [100 g] walnut halves

2 Tbsp honey

FOR THE DRESSING:

1½ Tbsp red wine vinegar

1 tsp wholegrain mustard

1 tsp honey

1 Tbsp walnut oil

2 Tbsp extra-virgin olive oil

1. For the caramelized walnuts: Preheat the oven to 350°F [180°C]. Scatter the walnuts over a lined baking sheet, drizzle with the honey, and roast for 8 to 10 minutes until toasted and caramelized. Let cool, then break into small pieces.

2. For the dressing: Whisk together the vinegar, mustard, and honey, then gradually whisk in the oils. Season well with some salt and black pepper.

3. Slice the pears away from the core, toss with the lemon juice, and set to aside.

4. Toss the salad leaves with 2 Tbsp of the dressing and divide between plates. Tuck the slices of pear and cheese in between the leaves and scatter over the walnuts and pomegranate seeds. Drizzle a little more dressing over and around each plate and serve straightaway.

Or you could try ...

Apple, pecan & dried cranberry salad. Replace the pears with well-flavored apples such as Cox's or russets, the walnuts with pecans, use maple syrup instead of honey in the dressing and for the nuts, and dried cranberries instead of the pomegranate seeds. Some very thinly sliced celery adds a nice extra crunch.

Beet grows pretty much all year round, so it's almost a constant fixture at our tea room. We think it's best roasted with a splash of balsamic—it gives a really deep, slightly caramelized flavor.

Orange-roasted beet salad with goat cheese & dill

SERVES 6 TO 8

2¼ lb [1 kg] small beet
(ideally multicolored)

grated zest and juice of
1 small orange

2½ Tbsp apple balsamic vinegar

5 Tbsp extra-virgin olive oil

1 tsp honey

2 garlic cloves, crushed

1 Tbsp chopped dill,
plus extra for garnish

5¼ oz [150 g] soft rindless
goat cheese, crumbled

½ cup [50 g] toasted walnut pieces
or skinned, halved hazelnuts

¼ cup [25 g] pumpkin seeds

salt and freshly
ground black pepper

1. Preheat the oven to 375°F [190°C]. Trim the stalks from the beet, peel, and cut into bite-size wedges. Place them in a small roasting pan.

2. Add the orange zest to the beet with 2 Tbsp of the juice, 1 Tbsp of the vinegar, 2 Tbsp of olive oil, ½ tsp salt, and some pepper. Toss together well, cover the pan tightly with foil, and roast for 45 minutes to 1 hour until just tender. Remove and let cool until cold.

3. Whisk the rest of the vinegar with the honey, then whisk in the remaining oil. Stir in the garlic and season to taste. Spoon the dressing over the beet with 1 Tbsp chopped dill and mix together well. Transfer to a shallow serving bowl, sprinkle over the goat cheese, nuts, pumpkin seeds, and extra dill, and serve.

Or how about ...?

Roasted beet, pomegranate, and arugula salad

Roast the beet as above but using lemon zest and juice instead of orange. Make a dressing of 1 Tbsp pomegranate molasses, 1 Tbsp lemon juice, 1 tsp honey, 1 small crushed garlic clove, and 3 Tbsp extra-virgin olive oil. Season well. Stir through the beet with ⅓ cup [50 g] toasted pine nuts, the seeds from 1 pomegranate, and 1 oz [30 g] arugula leaves.

When we were children, our mom was always urging us to eat our greens, often finding imaginative ways to sneak them into meals. We no longer need such encouragement, especially with delicious recipes like this.

Summer green tabbouleh

SERVES 6

½ cup [100 g] medium-grain bulgur wheat

2 Tbsp extra-virgin olive oil

7 oz [200 g] zucchini, cut into ½-in [1-cm] dice

5¼ oz [150 g] freshly podded fava beans

2¾ oz [75 g] fine green beans, trimmed and cut into ½-in [1-cm] pieces

⅔ cup [75 g] freshly shelled peas

1 romaine or Boston lettuce heart, finely sliced

2¾-oz [75-g] piece cucumber, peeled, seeds removed, and cut into small dice

The leaves from a small bunch of fresh mint, finely shredded

The leaves from a small bunch of Italian parsley, coarsely chopped

4 scallions, trimmed and thinly sliced

⅓ cup [50 g] toasted pine nuts

1½ to 2 Tbsp lemon juice

Salt and freshly ground black pepper

1. Put the bulgur wheat in a large bowl and cover with plenty of boiling water. Let soak for about 10 minutes, or until the wheat is just cooked but still a little al dente. Drain well, then spread it onto a clean dish towel and leave for 15 minutes or so, to remove as much of the excess water as you can.

2. Heat 1½ tsp olive oil in a pan, add the zucchini and some seasoning, and toss over high heat for 3 minutes until lightly golden brown and just tender. Spoon onto a plate and let cool.

3. Cook the fava beans in boiling salted water for 3 minutes until just tender. Scoop out with a slotted spoon into a colander, run under cold water, and let cool. Add the green beans to the water and cook for 3 minutes. Add the peas, return to a boil, and cook for 1 minute, then drain. Refresh under running cold water, then drain well. Nick the skins of the fava beans with your fingernail and pop the bright green beans out of their skins.

4. Tip the bulgur wheat into a large mixing bowl and stir in the zucchini, beans, and peas, lettuce, cucumber, chopped herbs, scallions, pine nuts, lemon juice, remaining olive oil, and plenty of salt to taste. Spoon onto a large serving plate and serve straightaway while the lettuce is still crunchy.

Why not try ...?

Serving this with some yogurt cheese (see page 14) or feta cheese, crumbled over the top. Or adding a bit of lovely asparagus when it's in season.

You can use any type of green leaf for this tart, but we favor ruby chard. With its striking red stalks and veins, it's always a talking point with visitors to our organic gardens.

Roasted squash, red onion, green leaf & cheese tart

SERVES 6 TO 8

2 small red onions

13¼ oz [375 g] prepared butternut squash, cut into 1-in [2.5-cm] pieces

2 Tbsp olive oil

10½ oz [300 g] chard or spinach leaves, large stalks removed and coarsely shredded

7¾ oz [225 g] well-flavored cheese, crumbled or grated

3 extra-large free-range eggs

1¼ cups [300 ml] heavy cream

Salt and freshly ground black pepper

FOR THE WHOLEWHEAT PIE DOUGH:

1¼ cups [150 g] all-purpose flour

½ cup plus 2 Tbsp [75 g] stoneground wholewheat flour

¼ cup [65 g] chilled butter, cut into small pieces

¼ cup [65 g] chilled lard, cut into small pieces

1. For the pie dough: Put the flours into a food processor with the butter, lard, and ½ tsp salt. Whiz together until the mixture looks like fine bread crumbs, then add 2 Tbsp cold water and blitz briefly until the mixture comes together in a ball. Turn out onto a lightly floured counter and knead briefly until smooth. Thinly roll out the dough on the floured counter and use to line a lightly greased 23cm loose-bottomed tart pan 1½ in [4 cm] deep. Prick the bottom here and there with a fork and chill for 20 minutes. Preheat the oven to 400°F [200°C].

2. Peel the onions, leaving the root end intact, then slice each one through the root into thin wedges. Put the squash and onion wedges into a roasting pan with the olive oil and some salt and pepper and toss together. Spread out in a layer and roast for 20 to 30 minutes or until just tender.

3. Line the pastry shell with wax paper and fill with pie weights. Bake for 15 to 20 minutes until the edges are cookie-colored. Remove the paper and weights and return to the oven for 5 to 7 minutes until the bottom is crisp and golden.

4. Meanwhile, heat a large pan over medium-high heat, add the chard or spinach leaves, and cook for 2 to 3 minutes until wilted. Tip into a colander and gently press out the excess liquid. Season lightly.

5. Remove the pastry shell from the oven and lower the oven temperature to 375°F [190°C]. Arrange the roasted squash, onion, green leaves, and cheese in the pastry shell. Beat the eggs and cream with some seasoning, pour over the filling, and bake for 30 to 35 minutes until set and richly golden on top. Serve warm.

These spicy fritters are a bit like Indian pakoras. They're ideal at lunchtime with a salad, as an appetizer before a curry, or you can make smaller ones and serve them as nibbles with drinks.

Carrot & cilantro fritters with green yogurt sauce

SERVES 4 (MAKES 12 LARGE OR 24 SMALL FRITTERS)

2 Tbsp [25 g] butter

1 bunch scallions, trimmed, cleaned, and thinly sliced

2 extra-large free-range eggs

1/3 cup [80 ml] whole milk

3/4 cup [90 g] all-purpose flour

1/2 tsp baking powder

1 tsp ground cumin

1/4 tsp turmeric powder

1/4 tsp cayenne pepper

3 cups [350 g] grated carrots

1/3 cup [25 g] finely grated Parmesan

1 cup [15 g] cilantro leaves, chopped

Sunflower oil, for shallow-frying

Salt and freshly ground black pepper

FOR THE GREEN YOGURT SAUCE:

7 Tbsp [100 ml] whole plain yogurt

1 garlic clove, crushed

1/4 tsp superfine sugar

1/4 tsp salt

3/4 cup [15 g] mint leaves

1 cup [15 g] cilantro leaves

1 Tbsp extra-virgin olive oil

1. For the green yogurt sauce: Put all the ingredients into a food processor and blitz until smooth. Spoon into a bowl and chill for 1 hour.

2. Preheat the oven to 225°F [110°C] and line a baking sheet with plenty of paper towels.

3. Melt the butter in a small pan, add the scallions, and cook for 1 minute until softened. Set aside. Beat the eggs and milk together in a bowl, then sift over the flour, baking powder, cumin, turmeric, cayenne pepper, and 3/4 tsp salt. Whisk together.

4. Pile the grated carrot in the center of a clean dish towel and squeeze out the excess liquid. Stir into the batter with the scallions, Parmesan, and cilantro.

5. Pour 1/2-in [1-cm] oil into a large, deep frying pan and heat it to 350°F [180°C]. Drop 4 large or 8 smaller spoonfuls of the batter into the oil and flatten the mixture slightly with the back of a spoon. Fry until crisp and golden brown—1 1/2 minutes on each side for larger fritters or 1 minute for smaller ones. Lift onto the paper-lined sheet and keep warm in the oven while you cook the rest. Serve warm with the green yogurt sauce.

This recipe was inspired by some very good little veggie pies we had at the original Bill's in Lewes, in the south of England. If you'd rather make one big pie, use a 9-by-1½-in [23-by-4-cm] loose-bottomed tart pan.

Beet, new potato & crème fraîche pies

SERVES 6

2 Tbsp [25 g] butter

1 medium onion, chopped

2 garlic cloves, crushed

7 oz [200 g] peeled waxy potatoes, cut into ¼-in [5-mm] thick slices

½ cup [120 ml] whole milk

½ cup [120 ml] crème fraîche

1 cup [125 g] coarsely grated Caerphilly, Cheshire, or Lancashire cheese

1 cup [125 g] coarsely grated cheddar

8¾ oz [250 g] large beet, peeled and coarsely grated

¾ oz [20 g] bunch chives, chopped

Salt and freshly ground black pepper

FOR THE PIE DOUGH:

Scant 2 cups [225 g] all-purpose flour

¼ cup [65 g] chilled butter, cut into small pieces

¼ cup [65 g] chilled lard, cut into small pieces

1. For the pie dough: Sift the flour and ½ tsp salt into a food processor, add the butter and lard, and whiz briefly until the mixture looks like fine bread crumbs. Add 2 Tbsp cold water and blitz until the mixture comes together into a ball. Tip out onto a lightly floured counter and knead briefly until smooth, then divide into 6 pieces. Roll out into 6-in [15-cm] disks and use to line 6 lightly buttered 4-in [10-cm] tart pans, 1¼ in [3 cm] deep. Prick the bottoms here and there with a fork and chill for 20 minutes.

2. Preheat the oven to 400°F [200°C]. Line the pastry shells with foil and fill with pie weights. Place on a baking sheet and bake for 15 minutes until the edges are cookie-colored. Remove the foil and weights and return the shells to the oven for 5 to 7 minutes until the bottoms are crisp and golden. Set aside.

3. For the filling: Melt the butter in a large pan, add the onion, cover, and cook over low heat for 10 minutes until soft and lightly browned. Uncover, add the garlic, and cook for 1 minute more. Add the potatoes, milk, crème fraîche, ½ tsp salt, and some black pepper and simmer gently for 15 to 20 minutes, stirring regularly, until the potatoes are tender. (Watch they don't catch on the bottom of the pan.)

4. Remove the pan from the heat and stir in ⅔ cup [75 g] of each of the grated cheeses, the beet, and chives. Season to taste. Spoon the mixture into the pastry shells and sprinkle with the remaining cheese. Bake for 10 minutes until the cheese is melted and bubbling.

We normally make this with a good quality cheddar. Serve it with a simple salad, or as a side dish for roast chicken or lamb.

Or you could try ...? Eggplant gratin. Replace the zucchini and peppers with 2 large eggplants, cut across into ½-in [1-cm] thick slices and griddled until golden as below.

Zucchini, tomato & roasted red pepper gratin

SERVES 4

2 small red bell peppers

1 Tbsp [15 g] butter

1 large garlic clove, crushed

1¼ lb [600 g] canned plum tomatoes

1 Tbsp fresh oregano leaves

1 lb 10 oz [750 g] large zucchini, cut into ¼-in [5 to 6-mm] thick slices

2 Tbsp olive oil

1⅓ cups [150 g] coarsely grated cheddar

Salt and freshly ground black pepper

1. Preheat the oven to 425°F [220°C]. Put the red bell peppers on a baking sheet and roast in the oven for 20 to 25 minutes, turning them once or twice, until the skins are blackened in places and the flesh is soft. Seal them in a plastic bag and let cool. Then break them open, discard the stalk and seeds, peel off the skin, and tear the flesh into wide strips.

2. Meanwhile, melt the butter in a large, deep frying pan and add the garlic. As soon as it is sizzling, add the plum tomatoes and oregano. Bring to a simmer, breaking up the tomatoes with a wooden spoon, and let cook gently for about 40 minutes, stirring, until the sauce is really thick and beginning to stick to the bottom of the pan. Season to taste and spoon half over the bottom of a large, shallow baking dish.

3. Heat a large ridged griddle or grill pan until smoking hot, then lower the heat slightly. Toss the zucchini slices in the oil and griddle in batches for 2 minutes on each side, seasoning as you go, until marked with dark lines. Set aside on plenty of paper towels to drain.

4. Scatter half the griddled zucchini over the tomato sauce, followed by half the red bell pepper strips and half the grated cheese. Spoon over the remaining tomato then repeat the layers once more, ending with the grated cheese. Bake for 25 to 30 minutes until lightly golden and bubbling.

We always had great difficulty convincing our children to try cauliflower. That was before we came across this recipe for a jazzed-up cauliflower cheese. Now they complain that we don't make it often enough!

Cauliflower cheese with roasted cherry tomatoes & crispy bacon

SERVES 4

1 small onion, peeled, halved, and studded with 6 cloves

2 cups [500 ml] whole milk

3 large, fresh bay leaves

1/2 tsp black peppercorns

3 Tbsp [40 g] butter

1/4 cup [35 g] all-purpose flour

1 large, very fresh cauliflower, weighing about 3 1/4 lb [1.5 kg], core removed, cut into large florets

1 3/4 cups [200 g] coarsely grated sharp cheddar, plus more for the top

3 Tbsp heavy cream

2 tsp English mustard

7 oz [200 g] large, vine-ripened cherry tomatoes

1 tsp olive oil

12 slices rindless, smoked lean bacon

salt and freshly ground white pepper

hot buttered wholewheat toast, to serve

1. Pop the studded onion halves into a pan with the milk, bay leaves, and peppercorns. Bring to a boil, then remove from the heat and set aside for 20 minutes.

2. Return the milk to a boil, then strain it, discarding the flavoring ingredients. Melt the butter in a nonstick pan, add the flour, and cook over medium heat for 1 minute. Remove from the heat, beat in the hot milk, then return to a boil, stirring. Simmer gently for 5 minutes, stirring occasionally.

3. Meanwhile, preheat the broiler to high. Drop the cauliflower into a large pan of boiling water and cook for 7 to 8 minutes until tender. Drain well.

4. Remove the sauce from the heat and stir in 1 1/3 cups [150 g] of the cheese together with the cream, mustard, and seasoning. Toss the cherry tomatoes with the oil and season. Arrange the cauliflower in a shallow ovenproof dish and pour over the sauce. Scatter over the remaining cheese and tomatoes. Pop the bacon in a roasting pan, slide both under the broiler, and cook for 5 minutes, until the tomatoes are soft, the cheese is golden, and the bacon is crisp. Serve with toast.

Or how about ...?

Macaroni cheese. Cook 7 oz [200 g] macaroni in boiling salted water for 8 minutes until just tender, drain, and stir into the sauce. Spoon into the dish, and top with 3 thickly sliced tomatoes. Mix the remaining scant 1/2 cup [50 g] grated cheese with 1/2 cup [25 g] white bread crumbs, sprinkle over the top, and bake at 375°F [190°C] for 20 minutes until golden.

We're not normally huge fans of frozen veg, but with peas we make an exception. They're normally frozen within minutes of being picked, so they're actually far tastier than fresh peas that have been hanging around in the refrigerator for a while.

Warm lamb salad with a pea, mint & feta cheese dressing

SERVES 6

one 5½-lb [2.5-kg] leg of lamb, butterflied

2 Boston lettuces, broken into leaves, washed, and dried

¼ cucumber, halved and sliced

salt and freshly ground black pepper

FOR THE MARINADE:

6 Tbsp [90 ml] olive oil

the leaves from 2 rosemary sprigs, minced

the leaves from 2 large thyme sprigs, coarsely chopped

3 garlic cloves, crushed

finely grated zest and juice of 1 small lemon

FOR THE PEA, MINT, AND FETA CHEESE DRESSING:

3 small shallots, very thinly sliced

2 Tbsp red wine vinegar

¼ tsp superfine sugar

2¼ cups [250 g] frozen peas

8 Tbsp extra-virgin olive oil

the leaves from a ¾-oz [20-g] bunch fresh mint, chopped, plus extra whole leaves for garnish

7 oz [200 g] feta, crumbled

FOR THE GARLIC AND MINT YOGURT:

1 cup [250 g] whole plain yogurt

1 garlic clove, crushed

2 Tbsp extra-virgin olive oil

2 Tbsp minced fresh mint

1. Mix the marinade ingredients together in a large shallow dish with 1 tsp each of salt and freshly ground black pepper. Add the lamb and turn it over in the mixture a few times until it is well covered. Cover and let marinate for at least 4 to 6 hours, ideally overnight.

2. To make the dressing: Put the sliced shallots into a mixing bowl and stir in the vinegar and sugar. Set aside for at least 30 minutes so that the shallots can soften. Cover the peas with warm water and let them thaw, then drain well and set to aside. Preheat the oven to 400°F [200°C].

3. Pop a ridged cast-iron griddle or grill pan over high heat until smoking hot, then lower the heat to medium-low. Lift the lamb out of the marinade, shaking off the excess, then place it on the griddle, and cook for 5 to 7 minutes on each side until well colored. Transfer to a roasting pan, spoon over any remaining marinade, and roast for 20 to 25 minutes. Transfer the meat to a carving board, cover with foil, and let rest for 5 to 10 minutes.

4. Meanwhile, tear the lettuce leaves into smaller pieces and scatter them over the bottom of a large serving platter along with the sliced cucumber. Mix the yogurt ingredients together and season to taste.

5. Add the oil to the shallots and swirl together. Stir in the peas and mint and season to taste.

6. Carve the lamb across into thin slices and pop it on top of the lettuce. Spoon over the pea and mint dressing, sprinkle over the feta, and sprinkle with a few more small mint leaves. Eat straightaway with the garlic and mint yogurt.

Ooh, we do love a good frost. Now, that might sound a bit odd, but when you consider that veg like the wondrous curly kale taste so much sweeter after a frost or two, perhaps we don't seem quite so eccentric. Perhaps.

A hearty kale, white bean & sausage stew

SERVES 4 TO 6

4 Tbsp olive oil

3½ oz [100 g] smoked bacon strips or small pieces

1 medium onion, halved and thinly sliced

½ cup [100 g] dried white beans, such as lima beans, haricot, or cannellini, soaked overnight

the leaves from 1 large fresh thyme sprig

7 oz [200 g] really meaty pork sausages

1 Tbsp [15 g] butter

1 small carrot, peeled and diced

1 celery stalk, thinly sliced

1 small leek, trimmed, cleaned, and thickly sliced

1 garlic clove, crushed

12¼ oz [350 g] mealy potatoes, peeled and cut into small chunks

1¼ cups [300 ml] chicken broth, or ham broth (see page 114)

4¼ oz [125 g] prepared curly kale leaves (i.e. minus any thick, tough stalks, etc.), coarsely chopped into wide strips

salt and freshly ground black pepper

1. Heat half the oil in a large saucepan. Add the bacon and fry for a minute or two until lightly golden. Stir in the onion, cover, and cook over low heat for 10 minutes until the onion is soft and very lightly browned. Drain the soaked beans and add them to the pan with the thyme leaves and 2 cups [500 ml] cold water. Bring to a simmer, part-cover, and cook gently for 45 minutes to 1 hour until tender. Add ½ tsp salt and simmer for another 5 minutes. Tip into a colander set over a bowl to collect the liquor. Measure the cooking liquor and make up to 1¼ cups [300 ml] with water if necessary. Set aside.

2. Meanwhile, heat 1 Tbsp oil in a small frying pan. Add the sausages and fry them gently until nicely browned, then pop on a plate. Heat the remaining oil and butter in the cleaned-out bean pan. Add the carrot, celery, leek, and garlic, cover, and cook gently for 5 to 6 minutes. Uncover, add the potatoes, a pinch of salt, some black pepper, the bean cooking liquor, and broth. Bring to a boil, cover, and simmer for 10 minutes or until the potatoes are almost soft.

3. Meanwhile, slice the sausages across into ½-in [1-cm] thick slices. Uncover the soup, stir in the kale, and simmer for 5 minutes. Add the sausages and cooked beans and simmer for another 2 to 3 minutes, until the kale is tender and the beans and sausages have heated through. Season to taste and serve.

Or you could try ...

Making this soup with fresh British or Spanish chorizo sausage. It imparts a lovely spicy paprika flavor and red hue to the stew.

the farmyard

The aroma of an organic, free-range chicken slow-roasting in the oven is surely one of the greatest gastronomic pleasures. Bettered only, perhaps, by the eating of it. We've been keeping chickens for years here at the farm, and happy years they've been—both for us and the chickens themselves. They've got lots of space to run around, which they certainly seem to enjoy.

If you're ever unsure how fresh an egg is, try popping it in a tumbler of cold water. If it sits on the bottom in the horizontal position, it's very fresh. If it tilts up a bit to a semivertical position, it's probably up to a week old. And if it floats vertically, it's stale.

To get the most out of your bird, use the leftover carcass to make a first-rate broth —following the method on page 120.

Organic and free-range chickens get to do lots of the things they enjoy most: grazing, pecking the ground, scratching about … and even a spot of dust bathing.

We add crushed oyster shells to our chicken feed—it helps them to produce eggs with good strong shells.

On the farm, we've always used duck eggs in our baking, but recently we've discovered that they're also rather lovely in a salad. As you can see from Frank's expression, bottom right.

Farmer's salad of fried new potatoes, duck eggs & blood sausage

SERVES 4

12¼ oz [350 g] small, mealy potatoes

1 Tbsp [15 g] butter

7 Tbsp olive oil

One 7¾- to 8¾-oz [225- to 250-g] blood sausage, skinned and cut into 16 slices

7 oz [200 g] thick-cut smoked lean bacon, cut into short fat strips

1 small garlic clove, minced

2 Tbsp sherry vinegar

2 tsp honey

1 tsp wholegrain mustard

1 Tbsp good walnut oil

4 free-range duck eggs

7 oz [200 g] mixed salad greens (watercress, dandelions, arugula, baby leaf chard, and spinach)

Salt and freshly ground black pepper

1. Peel the potatoes, cut them in half lengthwise, then across into ¼-in [7-mm] thick slices. Drop them into a pan of boiling salted water and cook for 3 minutes or until just tender. Drain well.

2. Heat the butter and 1 Tbsp of the olive oil in a frying pan, add the potato slices, and fry until crisp and golden brown on both sides. Season with salt and pepper and transfer to a low oven to keep hot.

3. Add another Tbsp of oil and the blood sausage slices to the frying pan and fry for 1 minute on each side. Remove to a plate and keep warm.

4. Pour away all but 1 tsp of oil from the pan, add the bacon, and fry for about 4 minutes until crisp and golden. Set aside with the blood sausage.

5. Add 2 Tbsp of the olive oil to the bacon fat left in the pan with the garlic, sizzle for a few seconds then add the vinegar, honey, mustard, and walnut oil and whisk into a dressing. Season and keep warm.

6. Heat the remaining oil in a clean frying pan and fry the duck eggs until they are done to your liking, spooning some of the hot oil over the yolks as they cook. Meanwhile, arrange the salad leaves, fried potatoes, blood sausge, and bacon on 4 plates and drizzle over the warm dressing. Top with the fried eggs, season them lightly, and serve with fresh bread.

This tart is a like a cross between a traditional quiche lorraine, a soufflé, and a British egg and bacon pie. It's best served warm, straight from the oven, while it is still light and fluffy.

Souffléd egg & bacon tart

SERVES 6 TO 8

1 tsp sunflower oil

7 oz [200 g] thick-cut smoked lean bacon, cut into short fat strips

3 1/2 Tbsp [50 g] butter

2 Tbsp all-purpose flour

3/4 cup [175 ml] whole milk, warmed

Scant 1 cup [100 g] finely grated hard cheese, such as cheddar or Lincolnshire Poacher

5/8 cup [150 ml] heavy cream

1/4 tsp freshly grated nutmeg

3 large free-range eggs, separated

Salt and freshly ground black pepper

FOR THE PIE DOUGH:

1 3/4 cups [225 g] all-purpose flour

1/4 cup [65 g] chilled butter, cut into small pieces

1/4 cup [65 g] chilled lard, cut into small pieces

1. For the pie dough: Put the flour into a food processor with the butter, lard, and 1/2 tsp of salt and briefly whiz until the mix looks like fine bread crumbs. Tip into a mixing bowl and stir in about 2 Tbsp of water until everything comes together in a ball, then turn out onto a lightly floured counter and knead briefly until smooth. Thinly roll out the dough and use to line a lightly greased 9-by-1 1/2-in [23-by 4-cm] loose-bottomed tart pan. Prick the bottom with a fork and chill for 20 minutes.

2. Meanwhile, preheat the oven to 400°F [200°C]. Line the pastry shell with wax paper and fill with pie weights. Slide it onto a baking sheet and bake for 15 to 20 minutes until the edges of the dough are cookie-colored. Remove the paper and weights and return to the oven for 5 to 6 minutes until the bottom is crisp and golden.

3. While the pastry shell is cooking, make the filling. Heat the oil in a frying pan over high heat. Add the bacon and fry briskly until lightly golden. Set aside.

4. Melt the butter in a medium pan, add the flour, and cook for 1 minute. Remove from the heat and gradually stir in the warm milk. Return to the heat and bring to a boil, stirring continuously, until smooth. Add the grated cheese and cream and stir together, then add the nutmeg, bacon, and some salt and pepper to taste and let cool slightly.

5. Remove the tart shell from the oven and lower the temperature to 350°F [180°C]. Stir the egg yolks into the sauce. Put the whites in a large, clean mixing bowl and whisk them into soft peaks, then fold into the sauce. Pour the mix into the case and bake for 30 minutes, covering with a sheet of foil after about 20 minutes, until puffed up, set, and golden brown. Serve immediately.

The first time we tried these Scotch eggs they were a complete revelation. Forget the chalky yolks and soggy crumbs of those sad, store-bought versions. These beauties, with their supercrunchy coating, are a different thing entirely.

Herby Scotch eggs with sage & lemon

MAKES 8

8 large free-range eggs

2 Tbsp [30 g] butter

$^2/_3$ cup [100 g] minced shallot or onion

finely grated zest of 2 small lemons

½ tsp ground mace

2 Tbsp chopped fresh sage

1½ lb [700 g] good pork sausagemeat

Sunflower oil, for deep-frying

Salt and freshly ground black pepper

FOR THE BREAD CRUMB COATING:

Scant ¼ cup [50 g] all-purpose flour, plus extra for dusting

3 extra-large free-range eggs, beaten

2½ cups [150 g] fresh white bread crumbs or Japanese panko crumbs

1. Lower the eggs into a pan of boiling water and cook for exactly 7 minutes. Remove from the pan and plunge into cold water to stop them cooking, then peel.

2. Melt the butter in a medium frying pan, add the shallot or onion, and fry gently for 5 to 6 minutes until soft but not browned. Tip into a bowl and let cool. Add the lemon zest, mace, sage, sausagemeat, and some salt and pepper and mix together well. Divide into 8 equal pieces and roll each piece into a ball, using floured hands.

3. Lay a large sheet of plastic wrap on the counter and lightly dust it with flour. Lay a ball of the sausage meat on top, lightly dust with flour then cover with more plastic wrap and roll out into approximately a 5½-in [14-cm] disk. Wrap the sausagemeat around the egg and press the edges together to seal, making sure there are no gaps and cracks. Chill in the refrigerator for at least 15 minutes.

4. Meanwhile, heat some oil in a deep-fat fryer or large saucepan to 350°F [180°C]. Roll the Scotch eggs in the flour, knock off the excess then coat in the beaten egg, and finally the bread crumbs, pressing them on to give a good coating. Deep-fry for 8 to 9 minutes until crisp, richly golden, and cooked through. Drain briefly on paper towels and serve hot with a crisp mixed salad.

Crunchy parmesan & garlic "picnic" chicken

Children seem to love anything cooked in crunchy bread crumbs and we must admit, so do we ...

SERVES 8

2 garlic cloves, crushed

2 large free-range eggs

3⅓ cups [200 g] fresh white bread crumbs

7 Tbsp [100 g] butter, melted

1¼ cups [100 g] finely grated Parmesan

4 Tbsp chopped curly leaf parsley

Sixteen 3½-oz [100-g] free-range chicken drumsticks, skinned

4 Tbsp sunflower oil

Salt and black pepper

1. Preheat the oven to 375°F [190°C]. Beat the garlic, eggs, and ½ tsp salt together in a dish. Mix the bread crumbs and butter in another dish, then add the Parmesan, parsley, ½ tsp salt, and some black pepper. Dip the drumsticks one at a time into the egg mixture and then into the cheesy bread crumbs, pressing them on well with your hands. Set aside.

2. Heat the oil in a large, nonstick frying pan over medium heat. Add the drumsticks, 4 at a time, and fry gently for just 2 minutes until nicely golden underneath. Lift them carefully onto a rack placed over a large roasting pan, golden-side down. Transfer to the top shelf of the oven and bake for 30 to 35 minutes until crisp, golden, and cooked through. Serve hot or cold.

Cauliflower, caramelized red onion & Caerphilly cake

SERVES 10 TO 12

1 Tbsp dried cornmeal

2 Tbsp olive oil

2 large red onions, peeled leaving the root intact, and cut into wedges

1½ lb [700 g] prepared cauliflower florets (approx. 1 large cauliflower)

1¼ cups [150 g] self-rising flour

½ tsp turmeric powder

1½ tsp fennel seeds, crushed

10 large free-range eggs, beaten

5 Tbsp [75 g] butter, melted

1⅓ cups [150 g] grated cheddar

The leaves from ¾-oz [20-g] bunch Italian parsley, chopped

7 oz [200 g] Caerphilly cheese, crumbled

Salt and freshly ground black pepper

1. Preheat the oven to 350°F [180°C]. Dust a greased and lined 9-in [23-cm] clip-sided round cake pan with the cornmeal, leaving the excess covering the bottom.

2. Heat the olive oil in a frying pan, add the onions, and cook gently for 15 to 20 minutes until soft and nicely caramelized.

3. Meanwhile, drop the cauliflower florets into a pan of well-salted boiling water and cook for 8 to 10 minutes until tender. Drain well and let cool slightly.

4. Sift the flour, turmeric, and ½ tsp salt into a large mixing bowl and stir in the fennel seeds. Make a well in the center, add the beaten eggs, and whisk together until smooth. Stir in the melted butter, cheddar, red onions, cauliflower, parsley, 5¼ oz [150 g] of the Caerphilly, and pepper to taste.

5. Pour the mixture into the pan and scatter over the rest of the Caerphilly. Bake for 45 minutes until set, covering loosely with foil once nicely browned. Remove from the oven and let rest for 15 minutes. Carefully run a knife around the pan's edge, remove the cake, and serve warm, cut into wedges.

This recipe for onion and raisin chutney makes enough for about four 12 1/4-oz [350-g] jars, so you'll have leftovers long after the parfait has been polished off. No bad thing: it's delicious with everything from cheese to cold meats.

Chicken liver & cider parfait with sticky onion & raisin chutney

SERVES 8

1/2 cup [75 g] minced shallots

7 Tbsp [100 ml] Madeira

7 Tbsp [100 ml] ruby port

3 Tbsp cider brandy or Calvados

The leaves from 2 thyme sprigs

2 1/4 cups [500 g] unsalted butter

1 lb 10 oz [750 g] fresh chicken livers, trimmed

2 small garlic cloves, crushed

Pinch each of freshly ground nutmeg, cloves, cinnamon, and allspice

Salt and freshly ground black pepper

Small gherkins, radishes, and thin slices of toast, to serve

FOR THE STICKY ONION AND RAISIN CHUTNEY:

2/3 cup [100 g] raisins

1 1/4 cups [300 ml] ruby port

1/2 cup [120 ml] sunflower oil

3 1/4 lb [1.5 kg] red onions, halved and thinly sliced

1/2 cup [100 g] packed brown sugar

1/2 cup [120 ml] red wine vinegar

1. For the chutney: Put the raisins and port in a pan, bring to a boil, then set aside to soak. Heat the oil in a large pan, add the onions, and cook slowly for 30 minutes, stirring, until soft and starting to caramelize. Add the sugar and cook for another 30 minutes, stirring occasionally, until richly browned and caramelized. Add the boozy raisins and vinegar and cook for 30 minutes until quite thick. Season with 1/2 tsp salt and some pepper and spoon into hot sterilized jars. Cover with wax disks and seal.

2. For the parfait: Preheat the oven to 275°F [130°C]. Put the shallots, Madeira, port, brandy, and thyme into a small pan and simmer until syrupy and reduced by about three-quarters. Let cool. Meanwhile, melt 1 1/2 cups [350 g] of the butter and let cool slightly.

3. Put the chicken livers, garlic, shallot reduction, spices, 1 1/2 tsp of salt, and plenty of black pepper into a food processor and whiz for 1 minute until very smooth. With the machine still running, add the melted butter and blend for a few more seconds, then rub the mix through a fine strainer into a bowl.

4. Pour the mix into an oiled and paper-lined 9-by-3 1/2-by-3-in [23-by-9-by 8-cm] terrine dish or loaf pan and cover with a strip of buttered paper. Put it into a small roasting pan half-filled with boiling water, cover with foil, and cook for 45 minutes or until just set. Remove from the roasting pan and let cool, then chill overnight.

5. The next day: Gently melt the remaining butter in a small pan, then pour off the clear butter into a small pitcher, discarding the milky solids that remain. Pour the butter over the parfait and return to the refrigerator to set. To serve, lift the terrine from its dish and peel away the paper. Slice thinly and serve with the chutney, toast, gherkins, and radishes.

Roast chicken is one of our very favorite suppers, but it can be hard to get spot on. That's why we're such fans of pot roasting: it's supereasy and you end up with fabulously juicy breast meat.

Pot-roasted chicken with apples & cider

SERVES 4

1 Tbsp sunflower oil

One 3¼-lb [1.5-kg] free-range chicken

6¼ oz [175 g] thick-cut lean bacon, or ham steak, cut into short chunky strips

1 large onion, chopped

8 small garlic cloves, thinly sliced

2 good fresh rosemary sprigs, coarsely chopped

1 cup [250 ml] good-quality hard cider

⅝ cup [150 ml] good chicken broth

4 small dessert apples, such as Granny Smith

3½ Tbsp [50 g] butter, softened

2 tsp superfine sugar

a little freshly grated nutmeg

2 Tbsp all-purpose flour

2 Tbsp heavy cream

1 Tbsp chopped parsley

Salt and freshly ground black pepper

1. Preheat the oven to 350°F [180°C]. Heat the oil in a small ovenproof Dutch oven which will fit the chicken snugly. Season the chicken inside and out, put it in the Dutch oven, and brown it on all sides. Then lift it onto a plate, add the bacon, and fry until crisp and golden brown. Add the onion and cook over medium heat for about 5 minutes until soft, then add the garlic and rosemary and fry for another 2 to 3 minutes.

2. Add the cider and simmer vigorously until it has reduced by about three-quarters. Put the chicken back in the pan, pour over the broth, cover with foil, and pop the lid on. Cook in the oven for 1 hour.

3. While your chicken is cooking, peel, quarter, and core the apples and cut into thick wedges. Melt 2 Tbsp of the butter in a nonstick frying pan, add the apples, and fry them for a few minutes until they begin to brown. Turn the slices over, sprinkle over the sugar and nutmeg, and continue to fry for 2 minutes until they are just tender and nicely golden. Remove from the heat.

4. When the chicken is cooked, lift it onto a big cutting board, cover it tightly with foil, and let rest for 10 minutes. Put the pan over medium heat and simmer until the cooking juices are reduced and full of flavor. Mix the remaining butter with the flour, stir into the reduced juices, and simmer for a few minutes, stirring, until thickened. Mix in the heavy cream and season to taste. Stir in the parsley and apples. Carve the chicken and divide it between 4 nice warm plates. Spoon over the sauce and serve.

We adore coq au vin, but when cooking it ourselves, we like to keep the ingredients pretty local. So rather than a burgundy or a beaujolais, try a good local fruity red.

To make your own broth, pop the chicken carcass, wing tips, and giblets in a pan with an onion, a carrot, some celery, 4 bay leaves, a few peppercorns, and a thyme sprig. Cover with water, bring to a boil, then simmer for an hour. Strain and it's ready to go.

Chicken braised in local red wine with mushrooms & smoky bacon

SERVES 4 TO 6

1 tsp olive oil

7 oz [200 g] thick-cut, dry-cured, smoked lean bacon, cut into short thick strips

One 4½-lb [2-kg] free-range chicken, jointed into 8 pieces

7 Tbsp [100 g] butter

1 onion, halved and sliced

1 large carrot, peeled and sliced

1½ celery stalks, sliced

4 garlic cloves, sliced

4 Tbsp cider brandy or Calvados

1 bottle fruity red wine

Approx. 1¼ cups [300 ml] good chicken broth

2 Tbsp red currant jelly

1 Tbsp tomato paste

4 fresh bay leaves

1 large sprig thyme

10½ oz [300 g] baby carrots, trimmed

10½ oz [300 g] peeled button onions or small shallots

Pinch superfine sugar

8¾ oz [250 g] small cremini mushrooms

4 Tbsp all-purpose flour

Salt and freshly ground black pepper

1. Heat the oil in an ovenproof Dutch oven. Add the bacon and fry gently until crisp, then scoop out onto a plate. Season the chicken pieces, add them to the pan, and fry until nicely golden on all sides. Set aside.

2. Add 1 Tbsp [15 g] butter, the onion, carrot, celery, and garlic to the pan and fry until the onion is nicely browned. Return the chicken to the pan and turn up the heat. Pour over the cider brandy, set it alight, and wait for the flames to die down, then pour over the red wine and enough broth to cover. Add the red currant jelly, tomato paste and herbs, cover, and simmer for 1 hour, or until the chicken is very tender.

3. Meanwhile, melt 1 Tbsp [15 g] butter in a small pan, add the baby carrots and 2 Tbsp water. Season, cover, and cook gently for 6 to 8 minutes until tender. Heat 1½ Tbsp [20 g] butter in another pan, add the button onions, a pinch of sugar, and some seasoning, cover, and fry gently for 10 to 15 minutes until soft and golden.

4. Lift the cooked chicken pieces out with a slotted spoon onto a plate, cover, and keep warm. Strain the cooking liquid and return to the pan, skimming the excess fat from the surface, then boil rapidly until reduced to about 3 cups [750 ml]. Melt 2 Tbsp of the remaining butter in a pan, add the mushrooms, season, and toss over high heat for 2 to 3 minutes until lightly browned.

5. Mix the remaining 2 Tbsp [25 g] butter with the flour, whisk it into the sauce, and simmer for 2 to 3 minutes until nicely thickened. Return the chicken to the pan with the bacon and veg. Season to taste, heat through, and serve with buttery new potatoes.

When we we were growing up, Mom used to cook her roast chicken in one of those oval enameled dishes with a lid; it was always so wonderfully moist and tender. If you don't have one, a normal roasting pan and a sheet of foil like this works just fine.

Slow-roasted chicken with thyme, lemon & garlic

SERVES 4 TO 6

One 4½-lb [2-kg] chicken

1 lemon, halved

4 fresh thyme sprigs

4 fresh bay leaves

1 Tbsp sunflower oil, plus extra for roasting

The cloves from 1 small head garlic, separated but left unpeeled

15¾ oz [450 g] pork chipolata sausages

1 cup [250 ml] good chicken broth

1 Tbsp all-purpose flour

12 slices rindless lean bacon, rolled

Salt and freshly ground black pepper

FOR THE BREAD SAUCE:

1 onion, halved and studded with 15 to 18 cloves

2½ cups [600 ml] whole milk

1 fresh bay leaf

8 black peppercorns

1⅔ cups [100 g] fresh white bread crumbs

2 Tbsp [25 g] butter

2 Tbsp heavy cream

1. For the bread sauce: Put the onion halves, milk, bay, and peppercorns in a pan. Bring to a boil, then set aside to infuse. Preheat the oven to 375°F [190°C].

2. Pat the chicken dry and season inside and out. Stuff with the lemon, thyme, and bay leaves, truss the bird, and drizzle with oil. Put the garlic cloves in the center of a roasting dish or pan, pop the chicken on top, and add ¹⁄₁₆ to ⅛ in [2 to 3 mm] water to the pan. Cover with a lid or a large sheet of tented foil over the pan sealed to the edges. Roast for 1¼ hours.

3. Put the chipolatas into a small roasting tray with a little oil. Increase the oven temperature to 425°F [220°C]. Uncover the chicken and roast with the sausages for another 15 minutes until the skin is golden and crispy. Place the chicken breast-side down onto a carving board, cover with foil, and let rest for 15 minutes. Cook the sausages for another 10 to 15 minutes until golden brown. Bring the milk for the bread sauce back to a boil, then strain. Return it to the pan and stir in the bread crumbs and the butter. Set aside.

4. Meanwhile, preheat the broiler to high. Pour the excess fat from the roasting pan, put the pan over medium heat, and add a splash of broth. Rub the bottom with a spoon to release all the juices. Stir in the flour, cook for 1 minute, then gradually add the remaining broth, mashing the garlic as you go. Simmer for 5 minutes, then strain into a clean pan, season to taste, and keep hot.

5. Broil the bacon slices for 5 minutes, turning once until crisp. Uncover the chicken and pour any excess juices into the gravy. Reheat the bread sauce, stir in the cream, and season to taste. Carve the chicken and serve with the accompaniments and veg of your choice.

Now here's a recipe that could only come from England. Radishes, tomatoes, baby beet, scallions, cucumbers, new potatoes, lettuce: it's like an English garden on a plate.

Warm English chicken salad with tarragon salad cream

SERVES 6

One 3³/₄–lb [1.75–kg] chicken

1 quantity Tarragon & garlic butter (see page 17), softened

4 large, unpeeled garlic cloves, flattened under the blade of a knife

1 Tbsp olive oil

1 lb 2 oz [500 g] new potatoes

4 extra-large free-range eggs

the leaves from the center of 3 soft, round lettuces, separated

6 small, cooked beet, peeled and cut into wedges

¹/₂ cucumber, peeled, halved, and cut across into chunky slices

6 small, ripe, vine-ripened tomatoes, cut into wedges

1 bunch young scallions, trimmed and cut into 2

1 bunch small radishes, washed, trimmed, and halved lengthwise

salt and freshly ground black pepper

FOR THE TARRAGON SALAD CREAM:

scant ¹/₂ cup [150 g] mayonnaise

¹/₂ tsp English mustard

1 Tbsp tarragon or white wine vinegar

3 Tbsp light cream

1 Tbsp chopped tarragon

pinch superfine sugar

1. Preheat the oven to 400°F [200°C]. Flip your chicken onto its breast and, using poultry shears or kitchen scissors, cut along either side of the backbone. Open the chicken out, turn it breast-side up again, then press your hand firmly along the breast bone until it lies flat. Carefully push your fingers between the skin and the flesh, leaving the skin attached only at the end of each leg. Spoon small amounts of the butter evenly under the skin, pushing it into place from the outside. Secure the skin at the neck opening in place with a small, fine trussing skewer.

2. Scatter the flattened garlic cloves down the center of a lightly oiled roasting pan and place the chicken on top, skin-side up. Brush with oil, season, and roast for about 35 to 40 minutes, or until the juices run clear when the thickest part of the meat is pierced with a skewer. Lift the chicken onto a board, wrap it loosely in foil, and let rest for about 15 to 20 minutes until it is just cool enough to handle.

3. Meanwhile, put the potatoes into a pan of water, bring to a boil, and cook until tender. Put the eggs in a pan of simmering water and cook for 8 minutes. Mix the salad cream ingredients together.

4. Drain the potatoes and, when cool enough to handle, cut in half. Peel the eggs and cut into quarters. Pull the chicken meat away from the bones in large chunks. Scatter the lettuce leaves over a large plate and arrange the warm chicken, potatoes, eggs, beet, cucumber, tomatoes, scallions, and radishes in among the leaves. Drizzle over some of the salad cream and serve with the remainder in a separate bowl.

As much as we're partial to wild mushrooms (we do love a forage!), sometimes only a good old cremini mushroom will do. And this is one of those times.

Chicken & mushroom lasagna

SERVES 6 TO 8

9 sheets (about 6¼ oz/175 g) dried lasagna pasta

1 Tbsp olive oil

2 Tbsp [30 g] butter

10½ oz [300 g] cremini mushrooms, wiped clean and thickly sliced

the meat from 1 large roasted chicken (approx. 1¼ lb/600 g), pulled into chunky pieces

½ cup plus 2 Tbsp [50 g] finely grated Parmesan

FOR THE SAUCE:

1 small onion, peeled and halved

4 cloves

4½ cups [1 L] whole milk

2 fresh bay leaves

2 fresh thyme sprigs

1 tsp cracked black peppercorns

5 Tbsp [75 g] butter

½ cup [65 g] all-purpose flour

1½ tsp freshly grated nutmeg

3½ Tbsp heavy cream

1. For the sauce: Stud the onion halves with the cloves and put them into a pan with the milk, bay leaves, thyme, and peppercorns. Bring to a boil, remove from the heat, and set aside for at least 20 minutes to allow time for the flavors to infuse.

2. Bring a large pan of well-salted water to a boil. Return the milk to a boil, then strain through a strainer into a pitcher. Melt the butter in a medium pan, add the flour, and cook gently for 2 to 3 minutes without coloring. Remove from the heat and gradually stir in the hot milk. Return to a boil, stirring constantly, and let simmer gently over very low heat, stirring occasionally, for 10 minutes. Preheat the oven to 400°F [200°C].

3. Drop the sheets of lasagna pasta one at a time into a pan of boiling salted water, add the oil, and cook for 12 minutes or until al dente. Drain well, run briefly under cold water, then separate and lay them out side by side on a sheet of plastic wrap.

4. Stir the nutmeg and cream into the sauce. Melt the butter in a frying pan, add the mushrooms and some seasoning, and fry briskly over high heat for 3 to 4 minutes until all the excess moisture has evaporated. Stir them into the sauce with the chicken and some seasoning to taste.

5. Lightly butter an 8-by-11½-in [20-by-29-cm] shallow baking dish and line the bottom with 3 of the cooked lasagna sheets. Spoon over one-third of the chicken sauce and cover with another layer of the lasagna sheets. Repeat these layers once more, then spoon over the remaining sauce and sprinkle over the Parmesan.

6. Bake for 30 to 35 minutes, until golden and bubbling. Serve with a mixed leaf salad and hot garlic bread.

We have lots of ducks on the farm; they love our little pond. You can make this with wild mallard if you can get your hands on it, but it's just as delicious made with a duck from your local butcher or meat counter.

Pan-fried duck breasts with red currant & orange sauce

SERVES 4

2 large oranges

2 Tbsp superfine sugar

2 Tbsp red wine vinegar

⅝ cup [150 ml] good chicken or duck broth

1 Tbsp red currant jelly

1 Tbsp lemon juice

1 Tbsp orange flavored liqueur, such as Grand Marnier (optional)

¾ tsp arrowroot

scant ½ cup [50 g] fresh red currants, stripped off their stalks with a fork

four 6¼- to 7-oz [175- to 200-g] duck breasts

salt and freshly ground black pepper

1. Peel the zest from quarter of one orange and cut into long, fine shreds. Drop them into a pan of boiling water, leave for 5 seconds, then drain and refresh under cold water. Drain on paper towels. Squeeze the juice from both oranges and measure out ⅝ cup [150 ml].

2. Put the sugar and red wine vinegar in a small pan over low heat, stirring once or twice, until the sugar has dissolved. Increase the heat and boil vigorously until the syrup has turned an amber-colored caramel. Carefully add the broth, red currant jelly, and orange juice, bring to a boil, and let simmer until it has reduced by about half. Stir in the lemon juice, and orange liqueur. Mix the arrowroot with 2 Tbsp of cold water, add to the sauce, and simmer for 1 minute. Stir in the orange zest, season to taste, and keep warm.

3. Lightly score the skin of each duck breast into a diamond pattern, taking care not to cut into the flesh. Season the meat with salt and pepper and the skin with just salt. Heat a heavy frying pan over high heat. Add the breasts, skin-side down, lower the heat to medium, and cook for 4 minutes until the skin is crisp and golden. Turn the breasts over and cook for 5 minutes if you like your duck pink, or a little longer if you prefer it more cooked.

4. Pop the duck breasts onto a board, cover with foil, and let rest for 5 minutes, then slice them diagonally into long thin slices and lift them onto warmed plates. Stir the red currants into the sauce, bring it back to a simmer, then spoon it over the duck. Serve with peas, creamy mash, and a few green leaves.

... ...day after Christmas, our
... ould roast a goose for the whole
... wonderful tradition.

honey-roasted goose with spiced apple sauce & port gravy

SERVES 8

one 10-lb [4.5-kg] fresh, oven-ready goose, excess fat and giblets removed

1 small bunch fresh sage

3 Tbsp honey

salt and freshly ground black pepper

FOR THE PORT GRAVY:

1 small onion, coarsely chopped

1 carrot, coarsely chopped

2 Tbsp [25 g] butter

1 Tbsp all-purpose flour

5/8 cup [150 ml] ruby port

3 3/4 cups [900 ml] good chicken broth

FOR THE SPICED APPLE SAUCE:

3 1/2 Tbsp [50 g] butter

2 Granny Smith apples, peeled, quartered, cored, and coarsely chopped

1 large cooking apple (approx. 15 3/4 oz/450 g), peeled, quartered, cored, and coarsely chopped

finely grated zest of 1/2 small lemon

2 Tbsp superfine sugar

1/2 tsp freshly grated nutmeg

8 cloves

1. Preheat the oven to 425°F [220°C]. Season the cavity of the goose with salt and pepper, push in the sage, and tie it together with string. Season the skin with salt, place it on a rack over a large roasting pan, and roast for 30 minutes. Lower the oven to 350°F [180°C]. Remove the goose from the oven and pour the fat from the pan into a bowl. Return to the oven and roast for another hour, pouring off more fat after another 30 minutes. Remove from the oven, brush the skin with the honey, and return to the oven for a final 30 minutes. The goose will be done when the juices run clear when the thickest part of the leg is pierced with a skewer.

2. While the goose is roasting, make the gravy and apple sauce. Heat 1 Tbsp of the reserved goose fat in a medium pan, add the onion, and fry until well browned. Add the carrot, brown lightly, then stir in the butter and flour. Gradually add the port and broth and simmer vigorously until well-flavored and reduced to a good gravy consistency. Strain into a clean pan, season, and keep hot.

3. For the apple sauce: Melt the butter in a pan, add both types of apple, lemon zest, sugar, and spices, cover, and cook gently for 5 to 10 minutes until the cooking apple has reduced to a puree and the Cox's are tender. Season to taste and keep warm.

4. When the goose is cooked, strain any juices from the cavity into the gravy and put it onto a carving board. Cover with foil and let rest for 15 to 20 minutes. Arrange the meat on a large, warmed platter and serve with the apple sauce, gravy, and veg of your choice. To carve, slice off the legs, cut them in half at the joint and then slice the meat away from the bones. Slice the breast meat away from the carcass in two whole pieces and then carve each one lengthwise into long, thin slices.

the pastures

Someone once told us that the top six inches of soil supports all life on earth. (Thinking about it, it might well have been our school teacher!) Whoever it was, it really stuck with us and keeping our soil superhealthy, in a way that's completely sustainable, has always been at the heart of everything we do here at Yeo Valley. Well, we think it makes for far tastier dairy, not to mention meat ...

We like to think of our pastures as huge solar panels.

With the sun's help, clover-rich grass grabs nitrogen from the air and fixes it into the soil.

This superhealthy soil then repays us by growing top-notch grass for our animals to graze on.

Some salt beef needs a long soak before you cook it, so always check with your butcher. And don't throw away the precious cooking liquor, this makes a wonderful broth for a soup or stew.

Hot salt beef sandwich on rye with mustard & gherkin tartare & leaves

SERVES 8

Approx. 4½-lb [2-kg] piece unrolled salted brisket

2 carrots, halved

4 celery stalks, quartered

1 large onion, quartered

Small bunch parsley

Small bunch thyme sprigs

6 bay leaves

8 cloves

1 Tbsp cracked black peppercorns

FOR THE MUSTARD AND GHERKIN TARTARE SAUCE:

Scant ½ cup [150 g] thick mayonnaise

3½ Tbsp Greek-style yogurt

1 Tbsp English mustard

1¾ oz [50 g] finely chopped gherkins

Scant ¼ cup [25 g] capers, drained well and chopped

1 Tbsp chopped curly leaf parsley

½ tsp cider vinegar

TO SERVE:

1 rye loaf, sliced and buttered

Salad greens and sliced cucumber or pickled cucumbers

1. If necessary, soak the salt beef in cold water for 24 hours, changing the water regularly. Otherwise, simply rinse it well under running cold water.

2. Put the beef into a really large pan or ovenproof Dutch oven and cover by at least 3 in [8 cm] with cold water. Bring to a boil then reduce the heat to a very gentle simmer. The water should not be moving, with only a few tiny bubbles appearing from the bottom of the pan. (This is very important if you want to achieve meltingly tender beef.) Simmer for 20 minutes, then skim off the scum from the surface and add the rest of the ingredients. Simmer for another 2 hours 40 minutes, keeping the temperature consistent and topping off the water from a boiling kettle so that the beef remains well covered at all times. The beef is cooked when a fork will slide into the meat with little or no resistance. Remove from the heat and let the beef rest in the hot liquid for 30 minutes.

3. Meanwhile, mix together the tartare sauce ingredients. Spread a little of the tartare sauce on the buttered bread. Lift the salt beef onto a board and slice it thinly across the grain. Put some sliced cucumber, lettuce leaves, and hot salt beef onto half the bread slices. Place the remaining slices on top. Press down on each sandwich lightly, cut in half, and serve.

Our farm is just a stone's throw from the mighty Butcombe Brewery, where they make great ales. Any good brown ale or stout will do the job brilliantly here.

Braised steak in ale with a herby cobbler topping

SERVES 6

2¼ lb [1 kg] chuck steak, cut into 1½-in [4-cm] chunks

5 Tbsp sunflower oil

7 oz [200 g] smoked bacon pieces

2 cups [500 ml] good beef broth

2 Tbsp [25 g] butter

8¾ oz [250 g] small cremini or thickly sliced field mushrooms

2 medium onions, halved and thinly sliced

1 tsp white sugar

3 garlic cloves, crushed

2 Tbsp all-purpose flour

2 cups [500 ml] brown ale or stout

The leaves from 3 large thyme sprigs

4 fresh bay leaves

3 Tbsp Worcestershire sauce

Salt and freshly ground black pepper

FOR THE HERBY COBBLER TOPPING:

1⅓ cups [165 g] all-purpose flour

1 Tbsp baking powder

6 Tbsp [90 g] chilled butter, cut into pieces

1 Tbsp thyme leaves

1 Tbsp chopped curly leaf parsley

Scant ½ cup [50 g] finely grated cheddar

1 large free-range egg

2 Tbsp sour cream, heavy cream, or whole plain yogurt

Approx. 7 Tbsp [100 ml] whole milk

1. Toss the beef with plenty of seasoning. Heat 3 Tbsp of the oil in an ovenproof Dutch oven, add the bacon, and fry briskly until golden. Remove with a slotted spoon to a plate. Add the beef pieces in batches and brown well over medium-high heat. Spoon onto a plate.

2. Add half the broth to the pan and rub the bottom to release all the caramelized juices, then tip back into the rest of the broth. Add half the butter and the mushrooms to the pan and fry briskly for 1 to 2 minutes, then set them aside with the beef. Add the remaining oil and butter to the pan with the onions and sugar and fry them for about 15 to 20 minutes, stirring frequently, until richly caramelized. Add the garlic and cook for 1 minute.

3. Stir in the flour, followed by the ale, broth, thyme, bay, and Worcestershire sauce and bring to a boil, stirring. Return the beef, bacon, and mushrooms to the pan, season, and simmer for 1½ to 2 hours, stirring occasionally, until the beef is tender and the sauce has reduced and thickened. Remove the bay leaves and let cool slightly, then spoon into a shallow ovenproof dish. Preheat the oven to 350°F [180°C].

4. For the topping: Sift the flour, baking powder, and ½ tsp salt into a bowl, add the butter, and rub together until the mix resembles fine bread crumbs. Stir in the herbs and cheese. Break the egg into a measuring cup, add the cream, and make up to ¾ cup [180 ml] with milk. Stir into the dry ingredients, then spoon into separate mounds around the edge of the dish. Bake for 35 to 40 minutes until the cobbles are puffed up, golden, and cooked through.

... of
... tes.

...
thickly sliced on the diagonal

One 2-bone 6½-lb [3-kg] rib of
beef, chined but not trimmed

a little sunflower oil

2 Tbsp all-purpose flour

2 tsp English mustard powder

2 tsp freshly ground
black pepper

Salt and freshly
ground black pepper

FOR THE YORKSHIRE PUDDINGS:

Scant 2 cups [225 g]
all-purpose flour

½ tsp salt

4 large free-range eggs

1¼ cups [300 ml] whole milk

Beef drippings or lard,
if necessary

FOR THE GRAVY:

2 Tbsp all-purpose flour

2½ cups [600 ml] good beef broth

7 Tbsp [100 ml] red wine if you
wish, or more beef broth

...he oven to 450°F [230°C]. Spread the onion
...s over the center of a large roasting pan.
...int with a little oil, season the cut faces
... and pepper, and then score the fat in a
diamond pattern with a small, sharp knife. Mix the
flour, mustard, pepper, and ½ tsp of salt together
and pat the mix firmly onto the fat. Sit the joint on
top of the veg and roast in the oven for 20 minutes.
Lower the oven to 340°F [170°C] and continue to roast
the beef for another 1 hour 10 minutes.

2. Meanwhile, make the Yorkshire batter. Sift the flour
and salt into a bowl, make a well in the center,
add the eggs, milk, and ⅝ cup [150 ml] water and
beat to make a smooth batter. Leave for 30 minutes.

3. Transfer the beef to a board, cover with foil, and
let rest for 30 minutes. Increase the oven to 425°F
[220°C]. Pour the excess fat from the pan into a bowl
and make up to 2 Tbsp with melted beef drippings or
lard if necessary. Spoon ½ tsp of this fat into each
compartment of a 12-section muffin pan and heat
in the oven until smoking hot, then remove carefully
and fill each three-quarters full with the batter.
Return to the oven and cook for 25 to 30 minutes until
the Yorkshires are puffed up, crisp, and golden.

4. Meanwhile, make the gravy. Place the beef pan directly
over medium heat and when it is sizzling hot, stir
in the flour. Add a bit of the broth, scraping the
pan's bottom to release all the cooking juices, then
gradually add the remaining broth and the wine if
using. Bring to a boil, then simmer until reduced and
well-flavored. Strain, season to taste, and keep hot.

5. Uncover the beef, pouring any excess juices from the
board into the gravy. Carve into thin slices and serve
with the puds and gravy.

This is our version of a cottage pie, but made with all the flavors of a proper beef stew. Use good ground beef with at least 10% fat and don't be shy with the Worcestershire sauce.

Beef & barley cottage pie

SERVES 6

½ cup [100 g] pearl barley

2½ cups [600 ml] good beef broth

3 Tbsp sunflower oil

5¼ oz [150 g] lean bacon, finely chopped

1 large onion, minced

12¼ oz [350 g] carrots, peeled and finely diced

1 large celery stalk, finely chopped

2 garlic cloves, crushed

2½ lb [1.25 kg] good ground beef

1 Tbsp thyme leaves

3 Tbsp Worcestershire sauce

1 Tbsp tomato paste

2 tsp English mustard

⅝ cup [150 ml] red wine

Salt and freshly ground black pepper

FOR THE POTATO TOPPING:

1 lb 10 oz [1.75 kg] mealy potatoes, peeled and cut into chunks

5 Tbsp [75 g] butter

4 to 5 Tbsp sour cream or crème fraîche

A little freshly grated nutmeg

1. Put the pearl barley, broth, and ¼ tsp of salt into a small pan and bring to a boil. Cover and simmer for 25 minutes until tender.

2. Meanwhile, heat the oil in a large pan, add the bacon, and fry briskly until lightly golden. Add the onion, cover, and cook over medium heat for 5 minutes. Add the carrots, celery, and garlic, cover again, and cook for another 5 minutes until the veg are soft and lightly browned.

3. Add the ground beef, turn up the heat to high, and cook for 3 to 4 minutes, breaking up the meat with a spoon as it browns. Add the thyme, Worcestershire sauce, tomato paste, mustard, wine, cooked pearl barley, and broth and simmer for 25 to 30 minutes until the liquid has reduced and the mixture has thickened. Preheat the oven to 400°F [200°C].

4. Meanwhile, put the potatoes into a pan of salted water, bring to a boil, and simmer for 15 to 20 minutes until tender. Drain well, then return to the pan and mash until smooth (or pass them through a potato ricer). Stir in the butter and sour cream and season to taste with nutmeg, salt, and pepper.

5. Season the beef mix to taste and spoon it into a large ovenproof dish. Spoon the mash over the top, spread out evenly, and then rough up a little with a fork. Bake for 35 to 40 minutes until bubbling hot and golden brown.

Slow-roasted pork with butter-roasted apples, lemony carrots & cider gravy

SERVES 6 TO 8

2 tsp coarsely crushed
black peppercorns

1 Tbsp chopped rosemary

1 Tbsp chopped thyme leaves

1 Tbsp chopped sage leaves

3 large garlic cloves, crushed

1 Tbsp sea salt flakes,
plus extra for sprinkling

2 Tbsp olive oil, plus extra
for rubbing

One 5½-lb [2.5-kg] thick, boned
out piece of pork belly, skin
scored with a Stanley knife
at ½-in [1-cm] intervals

2 large onions, sliced

1 Tbsp all-purpose flour

⅝ cup [150 ml] heavy cider

⅝ cup [150 ml] good chicken broth

FOR THE BUTTER-ROASTED APPLES:

3½ Tbsp [50 g] butter

8 small dessert apples, peeled,
cored, and cut into quarters

4 tsp superfine sugar

¼ tsp freshly grated nutmeg

¼ tsp ground cinnamon

FOR THE LEMONY CARROTS:

1 lb 10 oz [750 g] carrots, peeled
and cut into small triangular chunks

2 Tbsp [25 g] butter

1 Tbsp superfine sugar

1 Tbsp lemon juice

1 Tbsp chopped parsley

1. Mix the peppercorns, chopped herbs, garlic, salt, and oil together into a paste and rub into the meaty underside of the pork. Set aside uncovered for 1 hour.

2. Preheat the oven to 450°F [230°C]. Spread the onions over the bottom of a large roasting pan and rest a rack over the pan. Put the pork skin-side up on top, rub the skin with oil, and sprinkle with salt. Pour ½-in [1-cm] of water into the pan, add to the oven, and cook for 10 minutes, then lower the oven to 340°F [170°C] and roast for 2½ hours, adding a little more water if necessary so that the onions don't burn.

3. For the apples: Melt the butter in a frying pan, add the apples, and fry over high heat, turning occasionally, until nicely golden. Add the sugar and spices, season, and toss together well, then tip into a roasting pan and roast in the oven for 15 minutes.

4. Remove the pork from the oven and raise the temperature back up to 450°F [230°C]. Put the onion pan to one side. Pop the pork back in the oven and roast for 15 to 20 minutes until the skin is crisp.

5. Cook the carrots in a pan of boiling salted water until just tender, then drain. Return to the pan with the butter, sugar, lemon juice, ½ tsp of salt, and some pepper and toss over medium heat for 2 to 3 minutes until well coated, then add the parsley.

6. Let the pork rest on a board for 10 minutes. Spoon the excess fat out from the onion pan, then place it over high heat. Stir in the flour, then the cider and broth and simmer until reduced and well-flavored. Strain and keep warm.

7. Carve the pork meat-side up into slices through the crackling. Serve with the apples, carrots, and gravy.

We make our own cider, and rather a lot of it.
As much as we love drinking the stuff, it's always nice
to save some for cooking. A big piece of ham poached in
hard cider really is a thing to behold.

Marmalade-glazed ham with chunky potato gratin

SERVES 8, PLUS PLENTY FOR CUTTING COLD

One 9-lb [4-kg] piece boned and rolled middle ham

At least 2.6 qt [3 L] dry, inexpensive hard cider

2 large carrots, peeled and quartered

2 large onions, peeled and halved

2 large celery stalks, quartered

12 cloves

2 tsp crushed coriander seeds

1 tsp cracked black peppercorns

a large sprig of fresh bay leaves

Salt and freshly ground black pepper

FOR THE SPICED MARMALADE GLAZE:

8 Tbsp fine-cut marmalade

6 Tbsp raw brown sugar

¼ tsp ground cloves

Approx. 40 whole cloves

FOR THE CHUNKY POTATO GRATIN:

2½ cups [600 ml] whole milk

2½ cups [600 ml] heavy cream

A little freshly grated nutmeg

4½ lb [2 kg] small, mealy potatoes, peeled and cut into ¼-in [5 to 6-mm] slices

1¾ cups [200 g] grated cheddar

1. Cover the ham in plenty of cold water and let soak for 24 hours, changing the water every now and then. To check it's ready, cut off a small piece of meat, cook it in simmering water for a few minutes then taste it. If it's still very salty, give it longer.

2. Put an upturned plate into a large, deep pan, add the ham, and cover it by at least 1¼ in [3 cm] with cold water. Bring slowly to a boil, then drain, add the cider, and top off with water if necessary. Return to a boil, add the veg, cloves, coriander seeds, peppercorns, and bay leaves, lower the heat until the water is at a slight tremble, and cook for 1½ hours. Check the ham regularly toward the end of the cooking time—it's ready when a skewer slides easily into the joint's center and is hot to the touch once removed. Set aside and leave the ham in the liquid until cool enough to handle, then lift it out, remove the string, and carefully peel away the skin without pulling away any fat.

3. For the gratin: Heat the milk and cream in a large saucepan, add the nutmeg, and season to taste. Bring to a boil, stir in the potatoes, and simmer gently for about 10 minutes, turning occasionally, until just tender. Tip them into two 1.9-qt [2.25-L] buttered shallow baking dishes, shake level, and cover with the cheese.

4. Preheat the oven to 425°F [220°C]. Lightly score the ham fat into diamonds with a sharp knife, then place in a foil-lined roasting pan. Mix the marmalade, sugar, and cloves and spread thickly over the ham, pushing a clove into the center of each diamond. Roast for 20 minutes or until the fat is a deep golden brown. Let rest for 20 to 30 minutes. Lower the oven temperature to 350°F [180°C], slide the gratins into the oven, and bake for 30 minutes until golden and bubbling. Carve and serve the ham with the gratin and a salad.

We'd recommend seeking out proper big chops for this recipe. They're much more likely to stay nice and juicy than the sad, thin ones you so often see around.

Sweet 'n' smoky pork chops with cabbage & mash

SERVES 4

4 large pork chops on the bone, cut 1 to 1¼ in [2.5 to 3 cm] thick, and weighing about 14 oz [400 g] each

2 garlic cloves

1½ tsp sweet smoked paprika

3 Tbsp olive oil

2 Tbsp cider vinegar

3 Tbsp honey or maple syrup

Salt and freshly ground black pepper

FOR THE CELERIAC MASH:

1¼ lb [600 g] celeriac, peeled and cut into chunks

10½ oz [300 g] mealy potatoes, peeled and cut into chunks

2 Tbsp [25 g] butter

FOR THE BUTTERED CARAWAY AND GARLIC CABBAGE:

1 pointed cabbage, weighing about 1 lb 10 oz [750 g]

2 Tbsp [25 g] butter

1 tsp caraway seeds

2 garlic cloves, crushed

1. Slice the rind from each pork chop, leaving behind all the fat, and lightly score the meaty surface on each side with a sharp knife. Flatten the garlic cloves under the blade of a knife, sprinkle with ½ tsp of salt, and crush them into a paste. Mix with the paprika, olive oil, vinegar, honey, and some black pepper. Rub the mixture over both sides of the chops, cover, and let marinate for 1 to 2 hours.

2. Preheat the oven to 425°F [220°C]. Heat a large frying pan over medium heat. Lift the chops out of the marinade and, using tongs, hold them one at a time on their sides, searing the fatty edge until crisp and golden. Then fry the chops for 2 minutes on each side until lightly browned. Transfer them to a lightly oiled roasting pan, pour over any leftover marinade, and roast them for 20 minutes until cooked through, but still juicy in the center.

3. While the chops are roasting, boil the celeriac and potatoes in well-salted water until tender—about 15 to 20 minutes. Drain well, return to the pan, and mash until smooth. Stir in the butter and season to taste.

4. Meanwhile, shred the cabbage into ½-in [1-cm] wide strips, discarding the core. Drop it into a large pan of boiling salted water, cook for 3 minutes, then drain. Melt the butter in a large pan, add the caraway seeds and garlic, and as soon as they start to sizzle, add the cabbage and toss over high heat for 1 minute until just cooked, but still slightly crunchy. Serve with the pork chops and celeriac mash.

This is a firm favorite with all our family, from the little ones right through to the oldies. The meatballs and the sauce freeze beautifully, so why not double the quantities and save half for a rainy day?

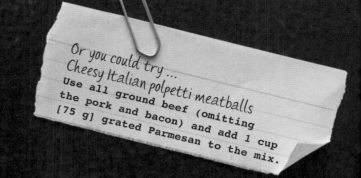

Or you could try ...
Cheesy Italian polpetti meatballs
Use all ground beef (omitting the pork and bacon) and add 1 cup [75 g] grated Parmesan to the mix.

Smoky bacon meatballs with pappardelle pasta

SERVES 4

14 oz to 1 lb 2 oz [400 to 500 g] dried pappardelle pasta

Salt and freshly ground black pepper

FOR THE MEATBALLS:

4 Tbsp olive oil

1 medium onion, minced

2 garlic cloves, crushed

7³/₄ oz [225 g] dry-cured, smoked lean bacon

1 lb 2 oz [500 g] ground beef

8³/₄ oz [250 g] ground pork

Finely grated zest of 1 small lemon

1¹/₄ cups [75 g] fresh bread crumbs

³/₄ oz [20 g] fresh oregano leaves

1 large free-range egg, beaten

FOR THE TOMATO SAUCE:

1 Tbsp olive oil

1 Tbsp [15 g] butter

1 medium onion, minced

2 garlic cloves, crushed

1 red bell pepper, stalk and seeds removed and flesh finely chopped

¹/₂ seeded and chopped red chile (optional)

7 oz [200 g] canned chopped tomatoes

12¹/₄ oz [350 g] strained tomatoes

1 Tbsp apple balsamic vinegar

1 tsp superfine sugar

A large handful of basil leaves

1. For the meatballs: Heat 2 Tbsp of olive oil in a small pan, add the onion and garlic, cover, and cook over low heat for 10 minutes until soft. Tip into a large mixing bowl and let cool slightly.

2. For the sauce: Heat the oil and butter in a large saucepan or ovenproof Dutch oven over low heat. Stir in the onion, garlic, pepper, and chile if using, cover, and cook gently for 10 minutes until softened. Uncover, add the chopped tomatoes, strained tomatoes, apple balsamic, sugar, ¹/₂ tsp of salt, and some black pepper and bring to a simmer.

3. Put the bacon into a food processor and pulse until finely chopped. Add to the mixing bowl with the ground beef, pork, lemon zest, bread crumbs, oregano, egg, ¹/₂ tsp salt, and plenty of black pepper and mix together well with your hands. Shape the mixture into walnut-size balls.

4. Heat the remaining 2 Tbsp of olive oil in a large, nonstick frying pan. Add the meatballs, a few at a time, and brown them all over, then drop them into the simmering sauce. When all the meatballs have been added, part-cover the pan and simmer gently for 20 minutes, stirring gently now and then so as not to break up the meatballs.

5. Meanwhile, bring a large pan of well-salted water to a boil. When the meatballs are ready, add the pappardelle and cook for about 12 minutes, or until tender but still a little al dente. Coarsely chop the basil and stir into the meatballs. Serve with the pasta.

You can make this with spring lamb, but we think it's worth waiting until the summer, when the lambs have had plenty of time to feed on fresh pasture. They give a far richer flavor with a little more age on their side.

Roast leg of lamb with rosemary & garlic "pesto"

SERVES 6

One 5-lb [2.25-kg] lamb leg

3¼ lb [1.5 kg] mealy potatoes, peeled

8 garlic cloves, peeled and halved

eight 2-in [5-cm] sprigs rosemary

3 Tbsp olive oil

2 Tbsp lemon juice

6 to 8 Tbsp [90 to 120 ml] good chicken broth

Salt and freshly ground black pepper

FOR THE ROSEMARY AND GARLIC PESTO:

3 garlic cloves, peeled

Sea salt flakes

The leaves from three bushy 6-in [15-cm] rosemary sprigs, minced

Finely grated zest of ½ small lemon

4 to 5 tsp olive oil

1. Preheat the oven to 450°F [230°C]. Using a small, sharp knife, make little 1-in [2.5-cm] deep slits all over the lamb leg, about 2 in [5 cm] apart.

2. For the pesto: Crush the garlic cloves on a cutting board with the blade of a chef's knife, then sprinkle with some salt and crush into a smooth paste. Mix with the chopped rosemary, lemon zest, some black pepper, and enough oil to make a paste. Push some of the paste into each slit, then rub the leg with the rest and season. Set aside at a cool room temperature for as long as you like. The longer you leave it, the more time the flavors will have to infuse the meat.

3. Cut the potatoes into roughly 1-in [2.5-cm] pieces. Put them into a large roasting pan with the halved garlic cloves, rosemary sprigs, olive oil, 1 tsp of salt, and some pepper, toss together well then spread out in an even layer.

4. Place a rack over the pan and put the lamb on top. Put it into the oven and roast for 15 minutes, then lower the oven temperature to 400°F [200°C] and roast for another 30 minutes.

5. Remove the pan from the oven and carefully lift the rack of lamb to one side. Loosen the potatoes from the bottom of the pan, sprinkle over the lemon juice and chicken broth, and replace the rack of lamb. Return it to the oven to cook for a final 35 minutes.

6. Remove the lamb from the oven, lift the meat onto a carving board, cover with a sheet of foil, and let rest for 15 minutes. Return the pan of potatoes to a low oven to keep hot. Carve the lamb into slices and serve with the rosemary and lemon potatoes.

Local farmers plough for victory at the 154th annual Mendip Ploughing Match, held right here on our farm. It really was a fantastic day, not least because of the obligatory ploughman's lunch followed by a spot of cider drinking.

We've always been big variety meat fans, but we know that some people aren't too keen. If you're one of them, this could be the recipe to convert you. It's certainly worked on guests of ours!

Griddled lamb chops with deviled kidneys

SERVES 4

8 lamb's kidneys

1½ Tbsp [20 g] butter, melted

¼ tsp cayenne pepper

1 tsp English mustard

½ tsp Worcestershire sauce

1 tsp lemon juice

1 Tbsp olive oil

8 loin lamb chops

1 Tbsp chopped parsley

Salt and freshly ground black pepper

FOR THE BROILED TOMATOES:

6 vine-ripened tomatoes, halved

2 tsp chopped thyme

1¾ Tbsp finely chopped pitted black olives

1 small garlic clove, chopped

1½ Tbsp [20 g] butter

1. Preheat the broiler to high. Put the tomato halves side by side in a shallow ovenproof dish and sprinkle over the thyme, olives, garlic, and some seasoning. Dot each one with a little of the butter.

2. Cut the lamb's kidneys in half and snip out the cores with scissors. Toss with some seasoning. Mix the melted butter with the cayenne, mustard, Worcestershire sauce, and lemon juice. Heat a large, ridged cast-iron griddle or grill pan over high heat until smoking hot, then lower the heat to medium-high.

3. Put the tomatoes under the broiler and cook for 8 minutes until tender. Meanwhile, brush the chops on both sides with a little oil and season well. Put them onto the griddle and cook for about 4 minutes on each side, until nicely browned on the outside but still pink and juicy in the center. Stand them on their fatty edges and cook for 1 minute more. Lift onto a plate, cover with foil, and let rest for 2 to 3 minutes.

4. When the chops are nearly cooked, heat 1 tsp oil in a frying pan, add the kidneys, and cook over high heat for 4 minutes, turning them over halfway through, until firm and lightly browned on the outside but still slightly pink in the center. Add the butter mixture and chopped parsley and toss together well over the heat for 30 seconds, but no longer. Serve with the chops and broiled tomatoes.

Most people love a good curry and we're no exception. We'd recommend cooking this one a day in advance and reheating it—the flavors get deeper as they get to know each other.

Our favorite Sumatran lamb curry

SERVES 6

1 lb 2 oz [500 g] onions

7 Tbsp [100 g] ghee or clarified butter

One 3¼-lb [1.5-kg] boned lamb shoulder

1 Tbsp cumin seeds

1 Tbsp coriander seeds

½ tsp cardamom seeds (not pods)

1 Tbsp sweet paprika

1½ tsp cayenne pepper

1½ tsp turmeric powder

½ tsp ground cinnamon

5 large garlic cloves

1¾-oz [50-g] piece peeled gingerroot, coarsely chopped

1 to 2 large red chiles, seeded

1 large red bell pepper, seeded and coarsely chopped

1⅔ cups [400 ml] coconut milk

1 Tbsp tamarind paste

Freshly chopped cilantro, to garnish

Salt and black pepper

FOR THE CUCUMBER AND MINT RAITA:

6¼-oz [175-g] piece cucumber

½ cup [125 ml] whole or Greek-style plain yogurt

1 tsp mint jelly, warmed

1 Tbsp chopped fresh mint

1. Thinly slice half the onions. Heat the ghee in a large, ovenproof Dutch oven, add the sliced onions, and cook over medium heat, stirring for 15 minutes until they are richly golden brown. Meanwhile, trim all the skin and excess fat from the lamb and cut the meat into ⅔ in [4 cm] chunks.

2. Put all the spices into a spice grinder (we have a coffee bean grinder reserved just for spices) or a mortar and pestle and grind them into a fine powder. Coarsely chop the rest of the onions and put them into a blender with the garlic, ginger, chiles, red pepper, spices, 1 tsp of salt, and 6 to 8 Tbsp [90 to 120 ml] cold water. Blend to a smooth paste, stopping and stirring the contents now and then to get the mixture moving if necessary. Add the paste to the fried onions and cook for 5 minutes more, stirring frequently.

3. Stir the coconut milk, tamarind paste, and lamb into the pan, cover, and simmer gently for 20 minutes. Uncover and continue to simmer for 1¼ hours, until the meat is tender and the sauce is thick. Adjust the seasoning to taste.

4. For the raita: Peel the cucumber, halve it lengthwise, and scoop out the seeds. Finely dice the flesh, toss it with ½ tsp of salt and leave it in a strainer to drain for 20 minutes. Dry it well on paper towels and mix with the remaining ingredients and a little more salt to taste. Season the curry to taste, scatter over a little chopped cilantro, and serve with some steamed rice and the cucumber raita.

the woods, hedgerows, fields & streams

We're incredibly lucky to have a lovely chap called Les Davies (MBE!) as our education officer.

He takes groups on tours of the farm and local woodlands. What he doesn't know about the Mendips isn't worth knowing!

Les's foraging top 10

wild garlic
field mushrooms
wild fennel
horseradish
crab apples
blackberries
elderberries
elderflowers
wild plums
damsons

JURASSIC

We believe that animals who lead healthy, happy lives make for better eating, which is why we love all things game. All that flying or running about in the wild means the muscles can develop naturally, so game is often both lean and extremely tasty. Slow cooking helps make it lovely and tender.

Remember to give your foraged fruits a good once-over for insects before you use them. Especially when cooking for vegetarians.

One of the best things about living and working in the valley is the wonderful food that surrounds us—and we don't just mean yogurt. The woodlands, hedgerows, fields, and streams are abundant with everything from fish and game to berries and mushrooms ... not to mention herbs. If you agree, why not put your boots on and see what you can find?

Wild garlic, with its large, glossy green leaves,
has to be one of our favorite things to forage for.
Next time you spy bluebells, have a closer look,
as there's often wild garlic nearby.
If you're uncertain, just follow your nose!

Spinach, wild garlic & phyllo pie

SERVES 4

Generous 1 cup [250 g] butter

10½ oz [300 g] feta cheese

½ cup [100 g] ricotta cheese

½ cup plus 2 Tbsp [50 g] finely grated Parmesan or pecorino romano

5 extra-large eggs

Scant 1 cup [50 g] fresh white bread crumbs

½ tsp freshly grated nutmeg

4 Tbsp extra-virgin olive oil

13¼ oz [375 g] fresh phyllo pastry, not frozen (approx. 14 12-by-15-in [30-by-38-cm] sheets)

7 oz [200 g] fresh spinach leaves, washed and dried well, tough stalks discarded, cut into ½-in [1-cm] strips

5¼ oz [150 g] wild garlic leaves, washed and dried well, tough stalks discarded, and leaves cut into ½-in [1-cm] strips

1 bunch scallions, trimmed and thinly sliced

Salt and black pepper

Top tip:

When wild garlic is not in season just use all spinach, and flavor the pie with a 1¾-oz [50-g] bunch of chopped mint or dill weed.

1. Put the butter into a small pan and leave over low heat until melted. Pour off the clear butter into a bowl, leaving behind the milky-white solids.

2. Crumble the feta into a large bowl and coarsely mash it with a fork. Add the ricotta, Parmesan, eggs, bread crumbs, nutmeg, oil, scallions, ½ tsp each of salt and pepper, and mix together well.

3. Preheat the oven to 350°F [180°C]. Lightly butter an 8-by-12-in [20-by-30-cm] roasting pan, 2 in [5 cm] deep. Unroll the phyllo pastry onto the counter. Set aside 7 sheets for the top and cover with a damp dish towel to prevent them drying out. Working as quickly as you can, brush one pastry sheet with the melted butter and pop it buttered-side down to line the bottom and sides of the dish, leaving about 2 in [5 cm] of the edges overhanging. Repeat this process with another 6 pastry sheets.

4. Add the shredded spinach and garlic leaves to the egg mix and stir together well. Spoon the mixture into the pastry-lined pan and spread it out evenly.

5. Butter one of the reserved pastry sheets and lay it buttered-side down over the pie, pressing it down well onto the top of the mixture. Repeat with the remaining 6 sheets. Press the overhanging edges together then trim to within 1 in [2.5 cm] of the edge of the dish. Lift them up and tuck them down the sides of the pie.

6. Using a sharp knife, mark the top of the pie into 8 pieces. Sprinkle with water and bake for 45 minutes until set in the middle, crisp, and golden, covering with foil if it starts to brown too quickly. Cool for 15 minutes. Cut into pieces along the lines and serve.

Taking the family mushroom hunting really is great fun. But always have an expert on hand, as you do hear horror stories. If you don't have a Les of your own, it might be best to head to your local farm shop or grocery store instead.

Field mushrooms in garlic & parsley butter on granary toast with crispy bacon

SERVES 4

2 fat garlic cloves

The leaves from 1 large thyme sprig

7 Tbsp [100 g] soft butter

2 Tbsp chopped curly leaf parsley

12 to 16 thin-cut slices rindless lean bacon or pancetta

4 large or 8 smaller thick slices of fresh granary or wholewheat bread

3 Tbsp olive oil

1 lb 10 oz [750 g] flat or closed-cup field mushrooms, wiped clean and thickly sliced

Salt and freshly ground black pepper

1. Pop the garlic cloves on a board and flatten them under the blade of a large knife. Coarsely chop the thyme leaves alongside them, then scoop them together, sprinkle with ½ tsp of salt, and crush together with the blade of the knife into a paste. Mix with the soft butter, parsley, and some black pepper.

2. Heat a large ridged cast-iron griddle or grill pan over high heat. Lay the slices of bacon side by side on the griddle and cook until crisp and golden—about 2 minutes on each side. Remove from the heat and keep hot. Toast the bread.

3. Heat a really large frying pan over high heat. Add half the olive oil and when it is jumping-hot, add half the mushrooms, season them lightly, and fry for just 2 minutes, tossing them until slightly browned but still firm. Add half the garlic butter and toss together briefly until the butter has melted.

4. Quickly put the toast onto warmed plates and pile over the mushrooms and their buttery juices. Top with the bacon and serve. Repeat with the remaining mushrooms for the other 2 portions.

Or you could try ...

Baked field mushrooms. Preheat the oven to 425°F [220°C] and put 8 large field mushrooms onto a lightly oiled baking sheet. Season lightly with salt and pepper, dot with the garlic and parsley butter, and bake for 10 minutes until tender. Squeeze over a few drops of lemon juice and serve with crusty bread.

After a bracing yomp in search of field mushrooms, there's no better way to warm up than with this simple and satisfying soup. Perhaps with some nice sourdough toast for dunking.

Field mushroom soup

SERVES 6 TO 8

1 oz [30 g] dried porcini mushrooms

7 Tbsp [100 g] butter

2 garlic cloves, crushed

1⅓ cups [200 g] chopped shallots or onions

the leaves from 2 large thyme sprigs

1 lb 10 oz [750 g] flat or closed-cup field mushrooms, chopped

the leaves from ¾-oz [20-g] bunch curly leaf parsley, chopped

2 Tbsp all-purpose flour

5 cups [1.2 L] good chicken or vegetable broth

⅝ cup [150 ml] crème fraîche or heavy cream

a little freshly grated nutmeg

salt and black pepper

1. Cover the dried porcini with ⅝ cup [150 ml] boiling water and let soak for 20 minutes. Meanwhile, melt 5 Tbsp [75 g] of the butter in a large pan, add the garlic, shallots, and thyme leaves, cover, and cook over low heat for 10 minutes until soft but not browned.

2. Drain the soaked porcini, setting the liquid aside, and finely chop. Add them to the softened shallots with three-quarters of the field mushrooms and fry for 5 minutes until the juices from the mushrooms start to run. Stir in the parsley and then the flour, cook for 1 minute, then gradually stir in the broth and all but the last Tbsp of the mushroom soaking liquid (which might be a bit gritty). Bring to a boil, lower the heat, cover, and simmer gently for 15 minutes.

3. Let the soup cool slightly then blend in batches until smooth. Stir in the crème fraîche or cream. Melt the remaining butter in the pan, add the rest of the mushrooms, season, and fry briskly over high heat for 2 minutes until they begin to color. Return the soup to the pan and simmer for 3 minutes. Season with nutmeg, salt, and pepper and serve with crusty bread.

Or how about ...?

Using wild mushrooms when in season. We like a mix of penny buns (ceps/porcini), hedgehog mushrooms (pied de mouton), yellow legs (winter chanterelles), flower of the wood (chanterelles girolles), horn of plenty (trompette de la mort), and oyster mushrooms. Chop the chunky ones but leave the little ones whole.

SERVES 10 TO 12

1 lb 10 oz [750 g] unskinned
trout fillets, pin-boned

2 Tbsp vodka

²/₃ cup [100 g] coarse sea salt

¼ cup plus 2 Tbsp [75 g]
superfine sugar

2 Tbsp finely crushed
white peppercorns

2 tsp crushed fennel seeds

1³/₄ oz [50 g] fennel herb or
dill weed, coarsely chopped

Finely grated zest of ½ lemon

Thin slices of rye bread or
pumpernickel, lightly buttered,
to serve

FOR THE MUSTARD AND
HORSERADISH SAUCE:

2 tsp finely grated
horseradish, fresh or
from a jar

2 tsp finely grated
onion or shallot

1 tsp Dijon mustard

¼ tsp English mustard powder

1 tsp superfine sugar

2 tsp white wine vinegar

5 Tbsp [75 ml] sour cream or
crème fraîche

5 Tbsp [75 ml] whole plain
yogurt

Salt

Trout & fennel gravlax with mustard & horseradish sauce

1. For the gravlax: Line a wide, shallow dish with
   plastic wrap and place half the trout fillets in a
   single layer, skin-side down in the bottom. Brush them
   with some of the vodka. Mix the salt with the sugar,
   peppercorns, fennel seeds, chopped fennel herb or
   dill weed, and lemon zest and spread over the top of
   the fillets. Brush the cut face of the remaining trout
   fillets with the remaining vodka and place flesh-side
   down on top. Cover with another sheet of plastic wrap,
   then place a board on top and weight them down with
   a few unopened cans. Refrigerate for 24 hours.

2. To serve: Remove the fish from the briny mixture,
   separate the pairs, and place skin side down on
   a board. Starting at the tail end, slice the fish
   away from the skin, sharply on the diagonal into
   thin slices as you would smoked salmon.

3. Mix the ingredients together for the mustard and
   horseradish sauce. Serve on top of the buttered
   bread, together with a small spoonful of the sauce.

Hyssop is a little-used herb that goes particularly well with pork, lamb, and fish such as trout. If you can't track it down, a mixture of mint and thyme works very well indeed.

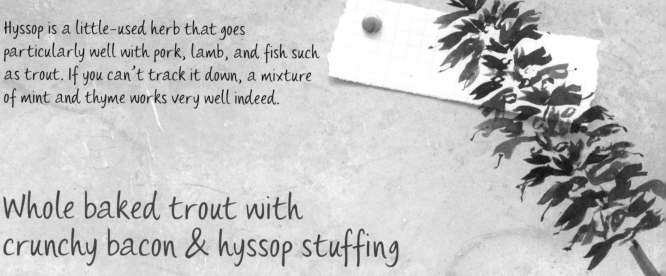

Whole baked trout with crunchy bacon & hyssop stuffing

SERVES 4

1 tsp sunflower oil

3½ oz [100 g] rindless smoked lean bacon slices, cut across into thin strips

5 Tbsp [75 g] butter

3½ oz [100 g] crustless white bread, cut into 1cm cubes

1 small onion, minced

3½ oz [100 g] cleaned and trimmed leek, thinly sliced

2 tsp chopped hyssop or mixed chopped mint and lemon thyme leaves

4 tsp chopped curly leaf parsley

1 large free-range egg

2 Tbsp whole milk

Four 10½-oz [300-g] trout

Salt and freshly ground black pepper

1. Preheat the oven to 400°F [200°C]. Heat the oil in a frying pan, add the bacon, and fry until crisp and golden. Remove with a slotted spoon to a mixing bowl, leaving behind as much of the bacon fat as you can.

2. Add 2 Tbsp [25 g] of the butter to the fat in the pan, leave until melted then add the bread cubes and toss together well. Fry over medium-high heat for about 5 minutes until crisp and golden. Season lightly with salt and pepper and add to the bowl with the bacon.

3. Add another 2 Tbsp [25 g] butter to the pan with the onion and fry gently for 5 minutes until soft and golden, then add the leek and fry, stirring, for 2 to 3 minutes more. Add to the bowl with the chopped herbs and a little more seasoning, mix together well, and let cool slightly. Beat the egg with the milk and stir 3 Tbsp of it into the stuffing mixture. Let soak for 5 minutes.

4. Melt the remaining butter. Season the gut cavity of each fish with salt and pepper, then spoon a quarter of the stuffing into each fish. Partly seal the opening with a small, fine skewer. Place the trout on a lightly buttered baking sheet, brush on both sides with melted butter, and season. Bake for 15 to 20 minutes until just cooked through. The flesh should be firm and opaque and should come away easily from the bones at the thickest part just behind the head. Serve straightaway.

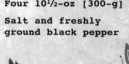

You can't beat a proper coarse farmhouse terrine, and this is one of our all-time favorites. Top tip: leaving the terrine to chill for a day or two after weighting it down lets the flavors develop wonderfully.

Or you could try ...
Gamey devils on horseback
Shape ⅓-oz [10-g] pieces of the terrine mix into little lozenges, then use them to stuff some soft, pitted prunes. Wrap each in half a stretched slice of lean bacon, pop on a baking sheet, and roast at 400°F [200°C] for 12 to 14 minutes, until golden. Serve hot with drinks.

Coarse game & green peppercorn terrine

SERVES 10 TO 12

2 Tbsp [25 g] butter

⅔ cup [100 g] minced shallot or onion

2 fat garlic cloves, crushed

3 Tbsp ruby port

3 Tbsp Madeira

1½ lb [700 g] mixed boneless game meat (an equal mixture of pheasant, rabbit, and venison), finely diced

8¾ oz [250 g] ground belly pork

The leaves from 2 large thyme sprigs

The leaves from two 6-in [15-cm] rosemary sprigs, minced

6 juniper berries, crushed then minced

½ tsp ground mace or freshly grated nutmeg

1 to 2 tsp green peppercorns in brine, drained, rinsed, and coarsely chopped

1 large free-range egg, beaten

10½ to 12¼ oz [300 to 350 g] dry-cured smoked lean bacon

8¾ oz [250 g] fresh duck or chicken livers, snipped into smaller pieces

Salt and freshly ground black pepper

1. Melt the butter in a small pan, add the shallot and garlic, cover, and cook gently for about 7 minutes until very soft but not browned. Add the port and Madeira and simmer until thick and syrupy. Let cool.

2. Put 7 oz [200 g] of the chopped game meat into a food processor and pulse until very finely chopped. Pop into a bowl and add the remaining game meat, pork, thyme, rosemary, juniper, mace, green peppercorns, reduced shallot mix, beaten egg, 1 tsp salt, and ½ tsp black pepper and mix together well with your hands. Chill overnight to let the flavors develop if you wish.

3. Stretch the bacon slices with the back of a kitchen knife and use to line the bottom and sides of a 2-lb [900-g] terrine dish or loaf pan, overlapping them slightly and leaving the ends overhanging. Press one-third of the terrine mixture into the pan's bottom and lay over a few pieces of liver. Repeat the layers once more, then finish with a final layer of the terrine mix. Fold the overhanging bacon over the top, sealing any gaps with 2 to 3 more slices if needed.

4. Preheat the oven to 340°F [170°C]. Cover the terrine with a lid or lightly oiled foil, pop it into a small roasting pan, and half fill with boiling water. Cook in the oven for 1½ hours or until the juices run clear when pierced with a skewer. Remove the terrine from the roasting pan and let stand for 15 minutes.

5. Pop a foil-wrapped piece of cardboard over the top of the terrine, weight it down with a few unopened cans, and let chill in the refrigerator overnight. Serve cut into slices with crusty bread, cornichons, and chutney.

Roasting pheasants is far easier if you do just hens or just cocks, that way all the birds will take the same time to cook. If you can, buy two brace and pop the spare birds in the freezer for next time.

Roasted pheasant with pearl barley & mushroom risotto

SERVES 4

2 plump, oven-ready pheasants, each weighing about 1 lb 10 oz to 1³/₄ lb [750 to 800 g], well-washed and any stray feathers removed

2 large thyme sprigs

2 Tbsp [30 g] butter

8 rindless slices dry-cured lean bacon

³/₄ cup [200 ml] fruity vintage cider

1 Tbsp crab apple jelly

⁷/₈ cup [200 ml] pheasant, game, beef, or roasted chicken broth

3¹/₂ Tbsp [50 g] chilled unsalted butter, cut into small cubes

Salt and black pepper

FOR THE PEARL BARLEY AND MUSHROOM RISOTTO:

1¹/₂ oz [40 g] dried porcini mushrooms

5 Tbsp [75 g] butter

1 medium onion, minced

1³/₄ cups [400 ml] pheasant, game, beef, or roasted chicken broth

1¹/₃ cups [300 g] pearl barley

13¹/₄ oz [375 g] wild or cremini mushrooms, cleaned and sliced

3 Tbsp chopped parsley

1 Soak the porcini in ⁵/₈ cup [150 ml] boiling water for 20 to 30 minutes. Drain, setting the liquid aside, then coarsely chop and set aside. Preheat the oven to 425°F [220°C].

2. Season the pheasant cavities with salt and pepper and stuff each with a thyme sprig and a little butter. Season the outside of the birds and truss them with string, then lay 4 bacon slices over each bird and pop them into a lightly oiled roasting pan. Roast the birds for 15 minutes, then lower the oven to 350°F [180°C] and roast for 15 minutes more, removing the bacon once it is crisp and golden and setting it aside. The pheasants are cooked when the juices run clear when pierced through the thickest part of the thigh.

4. Meanwhile, for the pearl barley risotto, melt 1¹/₂ Tbsp [20 g] of the butter in a small pan, add the onion, and fry gently for 5 minutes until soft and lightly golden. Add the porcini and fry for 2 to 3 minutes more. Add the broth and the pearl barley, cover, and simmer gently for 25 to 30 minutes until the broth has been absorbed and the barley is tender.

5. Transfer the cooked pheasants to a board breast-side down, cover tightly with foil, and let rest for 5 to 10 minutes. Pour any excess fat away from the juices left in the pan, place over medium heat, and add the cider, crab apple jelly, and broth. Boil rapidly until reduced to about 7 Tbsp [100 ml]. Strain into a pan, return to a simmer, and whisk in the chilled butter pieces a few at a time. Season to taste and keep warm.

6. Melt the remaining butter in a frying pan, add the mushrooms, and stir-fry for 3 to 4 minutes. Stir into the barley with the parsley and season to taste. Cut the pheasants in half along the breast and backbone and pop them onto warmed plates. Serve with the barley risotto, gravy, and some steamed broccoli.

There's something about getting out there and braving the elements that we really enjoy. Not to mention sitting down to a spot of steadying game pie afterwards.

Mixed game pie with sausagemeat-stuffing balls

SERVES 6

2 Tbsp sunflower oil

3½ Tbsp [50 g] butter

2¼ lb [1 kg] mixed boneless game meat (rabbit, pheasant, venison, and pigeon), cut into small chunks

7 oz [200 g] smoked dry-cured bacon, cut into chunky strips

1 large onion, chopped

The leaves from 2 thyme sprigs

1 tsp juniper berries, crushed

⅓ cup [45 g] all-purpose flour

2½ cups [600 ml] game, pheasant, roasted chicken, or beef broth

⅝ cup [150 ml] ruby port

1 Tbsp red currant jelly

4 bay leaves

2 carrots, peeled and diced

2 large celery stalks, sliced

1 Tbsp sunflower oil

Salt and black pepper

FOR THE STUFFING BALLS:

7¾ oz [225 g] pork sausagemeat

1¾ oz [50 g] rindless dry-cured lean bacon slices, chopped

2¾ oz [75 g] cooked and peeled chestnuts, chopped

Finely grated zest of 1 small lemon

½ cup [25 g] fresh bread crumbs

1 Tbsp chopped thyme leaves

Freshly grated nutmeg

FOR THE PIE DOUGH:

3 cups [350 g] all-purpose flour

6 Tbsp [90 g] chilled butter

6 Tbsp [90 g] chilled lard

1 large free-range egg, beaten

1. Heat the oil and 1 Tbsp [15 g] of the butter in an ovenproof Dutch oven. Brown the meat in batches, followed by the bacon and set aside on a plate. Add another 1 Tbsp butter [15 g] to the pan with the onion, thyme, and juniper and fry for 5 minutes until soft and lightly browned. Stir in the flour, then gradually add the broth, port, red currant jelly, and bay leaves. Bring to a boil, stirring, then return the game and bacon, cover, and let simmer gently for 1 hour.

2. Heat the remaining butter in a pan, add the carrots and celery, and fry gently until lightly browned. Add to the Dutch oven, and cook, covered for another 15 minutes, until the game and veg are tender.

3. Meanwhile, mix the ingredients for the stuffing balls together with some seasoning and shape into about 15 walnut-size balls. Heat the sunflower oil in a frying pan and brown them lightly on all sides.

4. Using a slotted spoon, transfer the meat from the game mix into a deep, rimmed 2.2-qt [2.5-L] pie dish. Reduce the cooking liquid to 2 cups [500 ml], pour back over the meat, and let cool. Pop a pie funnel into the center, then arrange the stuffing balls on top. Preheat the oven to 425°F [220°C].

5. For the pie dough: Sift the flour and 1 tsp salt into a food processor, add the butter and lard, and whiz until it resembles fine bread crumbs. Add 3 Tbsp cold water and whiz until it comes together into a ball, then turn onto a lightly floured counter and knead until smooth. Roll the dough out until 1 in [2.5 cm] larger than the top of the pie dish, then cut a small cross in the center. Cut a thin strip from around the edge of the dough, brush with beaten egg, and press onto the rim. Brush with more egg, then carefully lift the dough onto the dish so that the funnel pokes through the cross. Seal the edges and trim away any excess dough. Crimp the edges between your fingers, brush with more beaten egg, and chill for 20 to 30 minutes, then brush again and bake for 30 to 35 minutes until the dough is golden and the filling bubbling hot.

Or you could try ...
Beef stew with macaroni gratin
Switch the venison for chuck steak, adding the zest of ½ small orange and a cinnamon stick instead of the juniper. Omit the chestnuts and add 7 oz [200 g] browned white onions and ¼ cup [50 g] black olives instead. To serve, mix 1 lb 2 oz [500 g] cooked macaroni with 1 cup [250 ml] of the stew liquid and layer up in a gratin dish with 1 cup [75 g] grated Parmesan. Broil for 3 to 4 minutes until golden.

wine stew
with ne___ ___umplings

SERVES 6

3¼ lb [1.5 kg] trimmed venison shoulder, cut into 1½- to 2-in [4- to 5-cm] pieces

3 cups [750 ml] red wine

6 garlic cloves, crushed

1 tsp juniper berries, crushed then coarsely chopped

The leaves from 4 thyme sprigs

6 fresh bay leaves

3 Tbsp sunflower oil

4 Tbsp [60 g] butter

2 large onions, chopped

3 Tbsp all-purpose flour

2½ cups [600 ml] good beef, game, or venison broth

1 Tbsp tomato paste

2 Tbsp crab apple, red currant, or bramble jelly

7 oz [200 g] cooked peeled chestnuts

1 Tbsp apple balsamic vinegar

Salt and black pepper

FOR THE HERBY DUMPLINGS:

1¼ cups [150 g] self-rising flour

½ tsp baking powder

½ tsp salt

⅔ cup [75 g] shredded suet

The leaves from 2 thyme sprigs

1 Tbsp chopped curly leaf parsley

1. Put the meat, wine, garlic, juniper, thyme, and bay into a bowl. Cover and marinate for 24 to 48 hours.

2. Drain the venison through a colander set over a bowl. Lift out the pieces of meat and pat dry well on paper towels. Return all the herbs to the marinade.

3. Season the meat well with salt and pepper. Heat 2 Tbsp of the oil in a large ovenproof Dutch oven over medium-high heat and brown the venison in batches, spooning each batch onto a plate when done.

4. Pour away the excess oil from the pan, add the butter and onion, and cook over medium heat until soft and richly golden. Stir in the flour, followed by the marinade, bring to a boil, stirring, and let simmer vigorously until reduced by half. Add the venison, stock, tomato paste, crab apple jelly, 1 tsp salt, and plenty of black pepper and return to a boil. Simmer very gently, uncovered, for 1¾ hours, stirring occasionally, until the meat is almost tender and the liquid has reduced and thickened. Stir in the chestnuts and balsamic and season to taste.

5. For the dumplings: Sift the flour, baking powder, salt, and a little pepper into a bowl. Stir in the suet, thyme, and parsley, followed by approximately ⅝ cup [150 ml] water to make a soft, slightly sticky dough. Using a spoon, divide the mixture equally into 6 and drop, spaced apart, on top of the simmering stew. Cover and continue to simmer for another 20 minutes, until the dumplings have puffed up and are cooked-through and the meat is tender. A fine skewer pushed into the center of a dumpling should come out clean. Serve.

If you're using wild rabbit for this recipe, make sure to choose young ones as old rabbits can be tough as old boots. Farmed rabbit is delicious, too—look for "Label Rouge" as this is the mark of a happy bunny.

Braised rabbit with cider, mustard & crème fraîche

SERVES 4 TO 6

2 small young wild rabbits (each weighing about 13/4 to 2¼ lb/800 g to 1 kg) OR 1 large farmed rabbit (3¼ to 4½ lb/ 1.5 to 2 kg), jointed

2 Tbsp all-purpose flour

2 Tbsp sunflower oil

3½ Tbsp [50 g] butter

2 Tbsp cider vinegar

2 medium carrots, sliced

2 celery stalks, sliced

4 garlic cloves, sliced

The leaves from 1 large sprig thyme

The leaves from two 5-in [13-cm] sprigs rosemary, minced

1¼ cups [300 ml] dry fruity cider

1 Tbsp Dijon mustard

3½ Tbsp crème fraîche

1 tbsp chopped parsley

Salt and freshly ground black pepper

1. Season the rabbit pieces and dust them lightly with the flour, knocking off and seeting aside the excess. Heat the oil and half the butter in an ovenproof Dutch oven or deep-sided sauté pan until foaming, add the rabbit pieces, and brown them on all sides. Lift them into a shallow dish when they are done. Pour away the excess fat from the pan, add the cider vinegar, and scrape the bottom with a wooden spoon to release all the caramelized bits and pieces. Pour over the rabbit and wipe the pan clean.

2. Add the rest of the butter, carrot, and celery to the pan and fry for a few minutes until lightly browned. Add the garlic, thyme, and rosemary and fry for 1 minute. Stir in the reserved flour, then the cider, and return the rabbit pieces to the pan. Cover and simmer until tender; wild rabbit will take about 1 to 1¼ hours, farmed rabbit about 45 minutes.

3. Lift the rabbit into a warmed serving dish, cover, and keep warm in a low oven. Increase the heat under the Dutch oven or pan and simmer rapidly until the liquid is well-reduced and well-flavored—about 5 minutes. Stir in the mustard and crème fraîche and simmer a little longer until the sauce has thickened again. Season to taste, stir in most of the parsley, and pour over the rabbit. Sprinkle over the remaining chopped parsley and serve with some buttery mash.

The recipe for the beet relish makes a little more than you need for six burgers, but it'll keep in the refrigerator for two to three months and goes fabulously with cheeses and cold meats.

Venison burgers with apple balsamic & beet relish

SERVES 6

1 lb 10 oz [750 g] ground venison shoulder

8^3/$_4$ oz [250 g] ground belly pork

^{2}/$_3$ cup [100 g] minced shallots

The leaves from 3 thyme sprigs, coarsely chopped

Salt and coarsely ground black pepper

FOR THE APPLE BALSAMIC AND BEET RELISH:

^{5}/$_8$ cup [150 ml] cider vinegar

^{3}/$_4$ cup [200 ml] apple balsamic vinegar

^{1}/$_2$ cup [100 g] superfine sugar

1 large red onion, chopped

1 lb 2 oz [500 g] peeled raw beet, cut into fine matchsticks

1 large cooking apple

1 tsp lemon juice

Salt

TO SERVE:

^{1}/$_4$ cup [100 g] good mayonnaise

1 Tbsp grated horseradish, fresh or from a jar

6 floury baps or bread rolls

Lettuce leaves (red-tinged ones, such as ruby cos or oakleaf, look good)

^{1}/$_2$ cucumber, sliced

1. For the relish: Bring the cider vinegar, apple balsamic, and sugar to a boil, add the onion, and simmer for 5 to 10 minutes until just tender. Add the beet and simmer for 15 minutes more until tender.

2. Meanwhile, peel and coarsely grate the apple. Stir in the apple, lemon juice, and ^{1}/$_2$ tsp salt, bring to a boil, and simmer, stirring frequently, for about 10 minutes until the mixture has thickened and most of the excess liquid has evaporated. Let cool, then spoon into warm sterilized jars with vinegar-proof lids for keeping.

3. For the burgers: Put the ground venison and pork, shallots, thyme leaves, ^{3}/$_4$ tsp salt, and plenty of pepper into a bowl and mix together well. Divide into 6 and shape into ^{3}/$_4$-in [2-cm] thick burgers.

4. Barbecue or griddle the burgers over medium heat for 4 to 5 minutes on each side until nicely browned and cooked-through. Meanwhile, mix the mayo with the horseradish and a little seasoning. Split the rolls in half and spread the bottoms with mayo, then top with some lettuce leaves and cucumber. Pop the burgers on top of the lettuce, spoon over some beet relish, and sandwich with the roll tops. Eat straightaway.

Or you could try ...

Pheasant, juniper & celery burgers. Replace the
ground venison with ground pheasant, and use 2^3/$_4$ oz [75 g] ground bacon and 6 oz [175 g] ground belly pork. Add 1^1/$_2$ oz [40 g] minced central celery stalks to the mix and flavor with ^{1}/$_2$ tsp minced juniper berries.

We still get a thrill from picking what we call "hedgerow freebies." If you live in the city, you might well find elder trees in your local park. They flower late May to mid-June, so keep your eyes peeled!

Elderflower, rhubarb, and set creams

SERVES 8

FOR THE ELDERFLOWER
AND RHUBARB:

$7/8$ cup [200 ml] Elderflower cordial
(see page 187)

$3^1/4$ lb [1.5 kg] trimmed young pink
rhubarb, cut into $3/4$-in [2-cm]
pieces

$1^1/4$ cups [250 g] superfine sugar

$1/3$ oz [10 g] (about $5^1/2$ small
sheets) leaf gelatin

FOR THE ELDERFLOWER CREAM:

$1^1/4$ cups [300 ml] heavy cream

$1^1/4$ cups [300 ml] whole milk

$1/4$ cup [45 g] superfine sugar

6 Tbsp [90 ml] elderflower cordial

$1/4$ oz [6 g] (about 3 small sheets)
leaf gelatin

1. Put the elderflower cordial, rhubarb, sugar, and $5/8$ cup [150 ml] water into a large pan, cover, and cook gently over medium-low heat for about 5 minutes until the fruit is soft but not falling apart. Tip the mixture into a cheesecloth-lined strainer set over a bowl and let drain. You should end up with about $3^1/3$ cups [800 ml] juice. Set $1^1/4$ lb [600 g] of the cooked rhubarb aside in a mixing bowl.

2. Soak the gelatin in a bowl of cold water for 5 minutes. Warm $5/8$ cup [150 ml] of the rhubarb juice in a small pan and take it off the heat. Lift the gelatin out of the water, squeeze out the excess water, add it to the warmed juice, and let it dissolve. Stir this mix back into the rest of the rhubarb juice, then stir 6 Tbsp [90 ml] gently into the cooked rhubarb, setting the rest aside. Spoon the rhubarb equally into 8 glass tumblers, cover, and chill for 1 hour.

3. For the elderflower cream: Put the cream, milk, and sugar into a pan and warm very gently over gentle heat to dissolve the sugar. Put the elderflower cordial in a small pan and warm this gently too. Meanwhile, soak the leaf gelatin in cold water for 5 minutes, remove, squeeze out the excess water, and add it to the warmed cordial. Remove from the heat and let dissolve, then stir into the cream and milk.

4. Remove the tumblers from the refrigerator and pour over a layer of the cream. Chill for 2 hours or until set.

5. If the remaining rhubarb mixture has started to set, stand the pan in a little warm water until it dissolves again but don't let it get hot. Pour it over the top of the creams and chill one last time for at least 4 hours or until set.

Elderflower fritters with vanilla & honey yogurt

SERVES APPROX. 6

1²/₃ cups [200 g] all-purpose flour

1 large free-range egg, beaten

1¼ cups [300 ml] ice-cold sparkling water

1 Tbsp grappa, or any eau de vie (optional)

⁷/₈ cup [200 g] whole plain yogurt

The seeds from 1 vanilla bean

1 Tbsp honey

Sunflower oil, for deep-frying

18 to 24 heads of freshly picked elderflowers

Powdered sugar, for dusting

1. Sift the flour into a mixing bowl, make a well in the center, add the egg, and gradually whisk in the sparkling water to make a smooth batter. Whisk in the grappa if using. Cover and chill for 15 to 30 minutes.

2. Meanwhile, mix together the yogurt, vanilla seeds, and honey in a small bowl. Heat a large, deep sauté pan with enough oil for deep-frying to 350°F [180°C].

3. Grab the elderflower heads one at a time by their stalks, dip them into the batter, then shake off the excess. Separate the clusters if necessary. Holding onto the stalk, lower each fritter into the hot oil and press down gently so that the clusters splay out. Let fry for 1¹/₂ minutes, then flip over and fry for another 1¹/₂ minutes. Drain briefly on paper towels and dust lightly with powdered sugar. Serve with the vanilla and honey yogurt, but only dip sparingly or you will mask the flavor of the elderflowers.

Fall berry & apple batter pudding

SERVES 6

4 dessert apples, peeled, quartered, cored, and diced

Finely grated zest and juice of 1 orange

1 cup [185 g] superfine sugar

1¹/₂ lb [700 g] mixed blackberries and elderberries

2 Tbsp cornstarch, mixed with 2 Tbsp lemon juice

2 extra-large free-range eggs

1¹/₂ cups [175 g] self-rising flour

Pinch salt

7 Tbsp [100 ml] whole milk

7 Tbsp [100 ml] heavy cream

5 Tbsp [75 g] butter, melted and cooled

Powdered sugar, for dusting

1. Preheat the oven to 350°F [180°C]. Put the apples, orange juice, and ¹/₂ cup [110 g] of the sugar in a pan and simmer for 5 minutes until the apples are almost tender. Add the mixed berries and simmer for about 3 minutes more until the berry juices start to run. Stir in the cornstarch mix and simmer for a minute until thickened, then spoon the lot into a buttered, shallow, 2.1-qt [2.5-L] ovenproof baking dish and cool slightly.

2. Whisk the eggs and the remaining sugar together until thick and moussy. Whisk in the orange zest, then sift over half the flour and the salt and fold it in with half the milk and cream. Repeat once more, then fold in the melted butter.

3. Pour the mixture over the top of the berries and bake for 30 minutes until the pudding is firm to the touch and golden brown. Let cool slightly, then dust with powdered sugar and serve warm with yogurt, clotted cream, custard, or ice cream.

Wild plums and damsons are not always easy to get hold of, but this fool works equally well with ordinary plums. Just make sure you pit them and cut them into wedges before cooking.

Wild plum or damson fool with sponge fingers

SERVES 4 TO 6

10½ oz [300 g] wild plums or damsons

¼ cup plus 2 Tbsp [75 g] superfine sugar

⅞ cup [200 ml] heavy cream

FOR THE CUSTARD:

2 extra-large free-range egg yolks

2 Tbsp superfine sugar

½ tsp vanilla bean paste or extract

7 Tbsp [100 ml] heavy cream

7 Tbsp [100 ml] whole milk

FOR THE SPONGE FINGERS (MAKES APPROX. 30):

3 extra-large free-range eggs, separated

½ cup [90 g] superfine sugar

½ cup plus 2 Tbsp [75 g] all-purpose flour

6 Tbsp powdered sugar

1. For the custard: Whisk the egg yolks, sugar, and vanilla together in a bowl until thick and pale. Bring the cream and milk to a boil in a nonstick pan, then whisk into the yolk mixture. Return the lot to the pan and stir over low heat until the mixture thickens and coats the back of a wooden spoon. Pour into a bowl and let cool, then chill for at least 4 hours.

2. Put the plums or damsons into a pan with the sugar and stir over medium heat until the juices start to run, then increase the heat and cook for about 5 minutes, stirring occasionally, until cooked. Rub the mixture through a strainer into a bowl. Cool, then cover and chill along with the custard.

3. For the sponge fingers: Preheat the oven to 350°F [180°C]. Beat the egg whites in a large clean bowl into soft peaks. Whisk in the superfine sugar, 1 tsp at a time, to make a stiff and glossy meringue. Lightly beat the egg yolks and gently fold into the meringue, then sift over the flour and fold in. Spoon the mixture into a pastry bag fitted with a ½-in [1-cm] plain tip and pipe ¾-in [2-cm] wide strips in 3- to 4-in [8- to 10-cm] long lines across 2 large lined baking sheets, leaving 2 in [5 cm] between each one. Dust with half the powdered sugar and let rest for 5 minutes, then dust with the remaining powdered sugar and bake for 10 minutes. Let cool, then store in an airtight tin until needed.

4. To serve: Whip the cream in a large mixing bowl until it just begins to form soft peaks. Gently fold in the custard and plum puree until only just mixed. Spoon into a serving bowl and serve with the sponge fingers for dipping.

Hedgerow cordial

This is a delicious way of using up foraged crab apples. Cooking apples work just as well, mind.

MAKES APPROX. 7 CUPS [1.75 L]

5½ cups [800 g] blackberries

4¼ cups [600 g] elderberries

1¼ lb [600 g] crab apples, washed and coarsely chopped (in a food processor using the pulse button is quickest and easiest)

Juice of 2 large lemons

Granulated sugar 3½ cups [700 g]

1. Pick over the fruit for leaves and bits, then pop them into a large pan with the lemon juice and 4½ cups [1 L] of cold water and bring slowly to a boil. Simmer for about 20 minutes until the fruit is very pulpy.

2. Let cool for 10 minutes, then tip into a large fine-mesh strainer set over a bowl and let drain, until the fruits have stopped dripping and have yielded about 4½ cups [1 L] of juice, about 2 hours.

3. Measure the syrup into a large, clean pan and add 3½ cups [700 g] of sugar to every 4½ cups [1 L] of juice. Stir over low heat until the sugar has completely dissolved. Pour immediately into warm sterilized bottles, leaving a ½-in [1-cm] gap at the top, seal, and store in a cool, dark place or the refrigerator for up to 6 months.

Elderflower cordial

Just the thing for a hot day. We like to dilute with fizzy water, add a sprig of mint and a slice of lemon. Heaven!

MAKES APPROX. 2.1 QT [2.5 L]

30 to 40 large elderflower heads

3 lemons

7½ cups [1.5 kg] granulated sugar

1¾ oz [50 g] citric acid

1. If absolutely necessary, briefly rinse the flower heads to rid them of any bugs and shake them dry (or whiz them in a salad spinner). Put them into a large heatproof bowl. Grate the zest from the lemons, discard the ends, and thinly slice the rest.

2. Put the sugar and 5 cups [1.2 L] water into a large pan and bring slowly to a boil, stirring to dissolve the sugar. Stir in the citric acid, cool for 1 to 2 minutes, then pour the hot syrup over the flowers and stir in the lemon zest and slices. Leave to go cold, then cover and let steep somewhere cool for 24 hours.

3. Strain through a cheesecloth-lined strainer and decant into sterilized bottles (leaving a ½-in/1-cm gap at the top). Seal and store in a cool, dark place or the refrigerator for up to 6 months.

the fruit garden

Our favorite apples for eating—and juicing—would probably be a Granny Smith, or a Rhode Island Greening.

Somerset has an ideal climate for growing lots of different fruits, but we're probably most famous four our nice, juicy apples.

Fruit trees can take a few years to get going, but it's worth the wait: they'll keep on giving year after year.

The fresher the fruit is, the better it will taste, and the better for you it will be. Assuming it's perfectly ripe, of course!

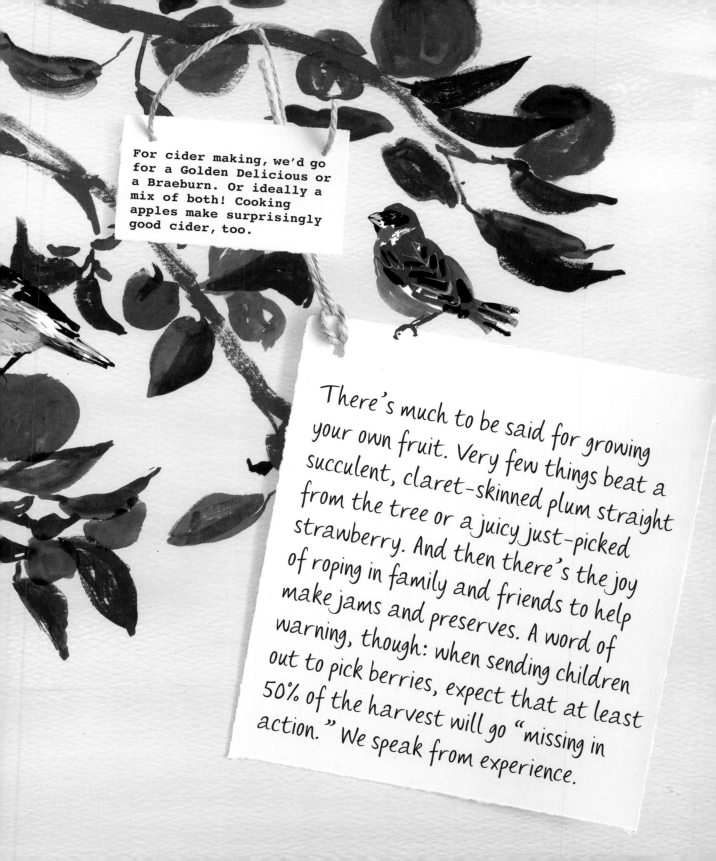

For cider making, we'd go for a Golden Delicious or a Braeburn. Or ideally a mix of both! Cooking apples make surprisingly good cider, too.

There's much to be said for growing your own fruit. Very few things beat a succulent, claret-skinned plum straight from the tree or a juicy just-picked strawberry. And then there's the joy of roping in family and friends to help make jams and preserves. A word of warning, though: when sending children out to pick berries, expect that at least 50% of the harvest will go "missing in action." We speak from experience.

Semifreddo is a delicious Italian-style ice cream. The secret is to take it out of the freezer a few minutes before you need it—that way it will be lovely and soft. This recipe's made extra special thanks to some limoncello and crumbled meringues.

Eton mess semifreddo

SERVES 8

2 cups [300 g] strawberries, hulled and halved

Finely grated zest of 1 small lemon

6 Tbsp limoncello or orange flavored liqueur

3 extra-large free-range eggs

1/4 cup [50 g] superfine sugar

1 1/4 cups [300 ml] heavy cream

1 3/4 oz [50 g] meringues (about 4 nests), crumbled into pieces

FOR THE STRAWBERRY SAUCE:

2 cups [300 g] strawberries, hulled

2 to 3 Tbsp powdered sugar, depending on the sweetness of the berries

2 tsp lemon juice

2 tsp limoncello or orange-flavored liqueur

1. For the semifreddo: Put the strawberries, lemon zest, and limoncello into a food processor and pulse into a coarse puree.

2. Separate the eggs into 2 large mixing bowls. Add the sugar to the yolks and whisk together until pale and really thick. Whip the cream in an third bowl until it forms soft peaks. Whisk the egg whites into soft peaks.

3. Gently fold the cream into the egg yolks, followed by the strawberry puree, egg whites, and crumbled meringues. Spoon the mixture into a 1.3-qt [1.5-L] shallow serving dish. Cover with plastic wrap and freeze until firm—at least 7 to 8 hours or overnight.

4. For the strawberry sauce: Simply puree all the ingredients in a blender until very smooth. Rub the mixture through a very fine strainer into a bowl, cover, and chill until needed.

5. Let the semifreddo soften slightly at room temperature before serving. Scoop large spoonfuls onto dessert plates and drizzle over the sauce. Serve quickly as this melts faster than normal ice cream.

Or you could try ...

Gooseberry and meringue semifreddo. Gently cook 2 1/4 lb [1 kg] gooseberries in a pan with scant 1/4 cup [40 g] superfine sugar and 6 elderflower heads until the juices run. Cover and cook for 5 minutes. Uncover, remove the elderflowers, and stir in another 1/3 cup to 1/4 cup, plus 2 Tbsp [65 to 75 g] sugar. For the sauce: Blend half the mixture until smooth, strain into a bowl, stir in 2 Tbsp elderflower cordial, and chill. Simmer the remaining berries for 7 to 10 minutes until a puree. Stir in 2 Tbsp elderflower cordial and let cool. Use the puree and sauce in place of the strawberry versions.

Sharing can be nice enough, but there's something to be said for having a pud all to yourself. Especially when it's this incredibly classy trifle, with its beautiful layers of fruit, custard, and brioche.

Summer pudding trifles

SERVES 4

²/₃ cup [75 g] black currants

Generous 1 cup [125 g] red currants, plus 4 sprigs to decorate

¼ cup plus 2 Tbsp [75 g] superfine sugar

1¼ cups [150 g] raspberries

¾ cup [100 g] small strawberries, hulled and cut into small pieces

2 Tbsp crème de cassis or crème de framboise (optional)

Half a 14 oz to 1 lb 2 oz [400 to 500 g] brioche loaf, cut across into 8 slices about ¼ in [6 mm] thick

7 Tbsp [100 ml] crème fraîche or lightly whipped cream, to decorate

FOR THE CUSTARD:

½ vanilla bean, slit open and the seeds scraped

5 Tbsp [75 ml] whole milk

5 Tbsp [75 ml] heavy cream

2 large free-range egg yolks

1 Tbsp superfine sugar

2½ tsp cornstarch

1. For the custard: Put the vanilla bean and seeds into a small pan with the milk and cream and bring to a boil. Set aside for 20 minutes to infuse. Whisk the egg yolks and sugar together until pale and thick, then whisk in the cornstarch. Return the milk to a boil, strain over the egg yolks, and whisk in. Return the mix to the pan and cook over low heat, stirring, until the custard is thick and coats the back of a spoon. Pour into a bowl and leave to go cold.

2. Put the black currants and red currants into a pan with the sugar and 1 Tbsp water and cook gently for 2 to 3 minutes until the fruit soften and just burst. Take off the heat. Blend 1½ Tbsp of the currant juice with ½ cup [50 g] of the raspberries until smooth, then rub them through a strainer into a bowl. Stir the raspberry puree back into the cooked currants with the rest of the raspberries, the diced strawberries, and the liqueur, if using. Tip the mixture into a strainer set over a bowl and let about three-quarters of the juice drain away.

3. Cut a disk from each brioche slice using a cookie cutter, so that they fit snugly inside your chosen dessert glasses. Spoon some of the fruit mixture into the bottom of each glass. Dip half of the brioche disks, one at a time, into the berry syrup until well soaked, then lay on top of the fruit. Cover with the remaining fruit mixture and then the rest of the syrup-soaked brioche slices.

4. Pour the custard evenly over the trifles and chill for 2 hours, or until the custard has set. Decorate with the cream and red currant sprigs before serving.

We're lucky enough to have a few pear trees on the farm, which is great as they're one of our favorite fruits to cook with. Like apples, they tend to go really well with spices.

Spiced pear bakewell

SERVES 8

FOR THE FILLING:

¾ cup [175 g] soft butter

Scant 1 cup [175 g] superfine sugar

2 extra-large free-range eggs

⅓ cup [40 g] self-rising flour

2 cups [175 g] ground almonds

1 tsp vanilla extract

1¾ oz [50 g] semisweet chocolate (about 70% cocoa solids), melted

2 ripe and juicy Conference or Bosc pears

¼ cup [25 g] slivered almonds

FOR THE PIE DOUGH:

2 cups [225 g] all-purpose flour

½ tsp ground cinnamon

Pinch salt

½ cup [65 g] powdered sugar

½ cup [125 g] chilled butter, cut into pieces

1 extra-large free-range egg yolk, beaten together with 4 tsp ice-cold water

FOR THE GLAZE:

½ cup plus 2 Tbsp [75 g] powdered sugar

¼ tsp ground cinnamon

1. For the pie dough: Sift the flour, cinnamon, salt, and powdered sugar into a food processor. Add the butter and whiz until the mix looks like fine bread crumbs. Pour over the egg yolk mixture and whiz again until it starts to stick together. Tip it onto a floured counter, bring together into a ball, and knead until smooth. Roll out and use to line a 9-in [23-cm] deep loose-bottomed tart pan, 1½ in [4 cm] deep. Prick the bottom with a fork and chill for 20 minutes.

2. Put a baking sheet into the oven and preheat it to 400°F [200°C]. Line the pastry shell with foil, fill with pie weights and bake for 15 minutes until the edges are cookie-colored. Remove the weights and foil and return to the oven for 5-7 minutes until the dough is crisp and golden brown. Set aside. Lower the oven temperature to 340°F [170°C].

3. For the filling: Beat the butter and sugar together in a bowl until light and fluffy. Beat in the eggs one at a time, adding 1 Tbsp of the flour with the second egg. Gently stir in the rest of the flour, the ground almonds, and vanilla extract.

4. Spread the melted chocolate over the bottom of the pastry shell. Peel, quarter, and core the pears and cut each piece lengthwise into 3 slices. Arrange them in a circle over the bottom of the shell. Spoon the almond mixture over the top and spread to the edges.

5. Put the tart onto the hot baking sheet and bake for 20 minutes. Carefully slide the oven shelf partway out and sprinkle the slivered almonds over the top. Slide it back into the oven and bake for another 30 minutes, covering loosely with foil toward the end of cooking if necessary, once it becomes browned. Remove and let cool, then carefully remove from the pan.

6. For the glaze: Sift the powdered sugar and cinnamon into a bowl and stir in 3 tsp warm water. Drizzle over the tart and let set before serving.

Why should the children have all the fun? Here are some truly decadent, grown-up desserts that look handsome served in wine glasses. Just the thing for a party. A light and fruity red would be perfect.

Black currant & wine desserts

SERVES 6

Scant 7¼ cups [800 g] black currants

1½ cups [300 g] superfine sugar

2 cups [500 ml] light and fruity red wine

½ oz [14 g] leaf gelatin (8 sheets)

Custard (see page 195) or ice-cold pouring cream, to serve

1. Put the black currants into a pan (there's no need to destalk them) with the sugar, red wine, and ⅞ cup [200 ml] water and slowly bring to a simmer, stirring to dissolve the sugar. Cook gently for 15 minutes. Then tip the mixture into a large, fine strainer set over another pan and let drain. This might take anything up to an hour, but don't squeeze out the juice or it will make your desserts cloudy. You should be left with 4½ cups [1 L] of intensely flavored juice.

2. Soak the leaf gelatin in a large bowl of cold water for 5 minutes. Put the black currant juice back over low heat and gently warm through. Lift the gelatin out of the water, squeeze out the excess water, and add to the pan. Stir until it has dissolved, then pour the mixture into 8 small dessert or wine glasses and chill for at least 6 hours or until set.

3. Pour some of the custard or cream on top of each dessert and serve.

Or you could try ...

Damson, red wine & cinnamon desserts. Replace the black currants with 2¼ lb [1 kg] damsons and add a 4-in [10-cm] cinnamon stick to the fruit, red wine, and sugar as they are cooking. Continue as before. These are nice served with lightly whipped cream, flavored with a little powdered sugar and ground cinnamon.

The mighty crumble. Does it get more British than this? It certainly doesn't get much more delicious—especially when it's made with juicy plums and crunchy hazelnuts. Not to mention clotted cream!

Plum, oat & hazelnut crumbles with clotted cream

SERVES 6

2 lb [900 g] plums

¼ cup [50 g] superfine sugar, plus extra to sprinkle

½ tsp ground cinnamon

1 Tbsp all-purpose flour

Clotted cream, to serve

FOR THE TOPPING:

½ cup plus 2 Tbsp [75 g] self-rising flour

½ cup plus 2 Tbsp [75 g] all-purpose flour

scant ½ cup [95 g] chilled butter, cut into small pieces

¼ cup [50 g] superfine sugar

2 Tbsp raw brown sugar

½ cup plus 2 Tbsp [50 g] organic rolled oats (ideally not jumbo oats)

⅓ cup [50 g] lightly toasted hazelnuts, coarsely halved

Pinch salt

1. For the topping: Put the flours and butter into a food processor and whiz until the mixture looks like bread crumbs. Add the superfine sugar and pulse briefly until the mixture starts to stick together, then tip it into a shallow dish or baking sheet. Add the raw brown sugar, oats, hazelnuts, and 1 tsp water and rake them through with a fork. Put in the freezer for 10 minutes or into the refrigerator until you're ready to bake.

2. Preheat the oven to 400°F [200°C]. Halve the plums, remove the pits, and cut the fruit into chunky wedges. Put the plums into a bowl with the sugar, cinnamon, and flour and mix together well, then spoon into six 9-oz [250-ml] deep baking dishes or mini ovenproof bowls.

3. Spoon the crumble mixture generously over the fruit but don't press it down. Put them onto a baking sheet and bake for 25 minutes until the fruit is hot and bubbling and the tops are richly golden. Remove and let sit for 5 minutes or so, then sprinkle with a little more superfine sugar and serve with some clotted cream dolloped on top.

Or you could try ...

Using any combination of seasonal fruits: 2 lb [900 g] fresh fruit pitted, peeled, cored, or destalked as necessary. Raspberry and apple is good, and so is peach and black currant. Ring the changes with the nuts in the topping (almonds are lovely with apricot) and flavors with the fruit, such as elderflower with gooseberry. The possibilities are endless! Only use the flour in the filling with really watery fruits.

Broiling fruit is a brilliant way to bring out the flavor and it always looks impressive with its lightly charred edges. You don't have to make the shortbread fingers, but they do lend a nice crunch.

Lemon posset with sugar-broiled apricots & shortbread fingers

SERVES 4

1¼ cups [300 ml] heavy cream

¼ cup plus 2 Tbsp [75 g] superfine sugar

Finely grated zest and juice of 1½ small lemons

FOR THE SUGAR-BROILED APRICOTS:

4 ripe apricots

The seeds from ¼ vanilla bean

2 Tbsp superfine sugar

FOR THE LEMON SHORTBREAD FINGERS:

1⅔ cups [200 g] all-purpose flour

½ cup [45 g] ground almonds

¼ cup [45 g] semolina or ground rice

¾ cup [200 g] chilled butter, cut into pieces

Finely grated zest of 1 large lemon

½ cup [100 g] superfine sugar, plus extra for sprinkling

1. For the posset: Put the cream, sugar, and lemon zest into a pan, bring to a boil, and boil for exactly 3 minutes. Take off the heat, stir in the lemon juice, then strain the mixture into a pitcher. Pour into teacups or ramekins and chill for at least 4 hours or until set.

2. For the shortbread: Preheat the oven to 340°F [170°C] and grease an 8-by-10-in [20-by-25-cm] shallow loose-bottomed pan and line the bottom with nonstick paper. Put the flour, ground almonds, and semolina into a food processor, add the cold butter and lemon zest, and whiz until the mixture looks like fine bread crumbs. Add the sugar and whiz briefly once more until the mixture just starts to stick together.

3. Tip the mixture into the pan and press out in an even layer. Bake for 25 to 30 minutes until a pale golden brown. Remove, mark the shortbread into 32 thin fingers, sprinkle generously with superfine sugar, and let cool. When cold, remove from the pan and carefully cut into fingers using a sharp, serrated knife.

4. Shortly before serving, preheat your broiler as high as it will go. Halve the apricots, discard the pits, and cut them into chunky wedges. Place them cut-side up on a baking sheet. Mix the vanilla seeds into the sugar with your fingertips and then sprinkle a little over each apricot piece. Slide under the broiler, as close to the heat source as you can, and broil for 3 minutes until they are hot and the sugar has started to caramelize. Put the apricots on top of the lemon possets and serve with the shortbread fingers.

Our farm cider ...

starts with 100% apple juice. You can make cider from one single variety apple, but we like to use a mix. That way we get a nice, balanced drink that's not too tart and not too sweet. The main three cider apples we use are Golden Delicious, Braeburn, and Granny Smith. Not that dessert or eating apples don't make good cider too—they do!

1. Pick apples at their ripest, when they start to fall from tree.

2. Mulch the apples. This means chopping them up quite coarsely and we have a machine that does this.

3. Place the pummace (the chopped apples) in cloths and layer them between the wooden slats of an apple press, until there are about 5 layers.

4. Apply pressure to squeeze out the juice, collecting it in a bucket placed below the press.

5. Decant the juice into barrels and leave the tops open. During this time the natural yeasts from the apples will start the fermentation process.

6. When the juice starts to ferment, a frothy scum develops on the surface. We scrape this off each day and top off the liquid level with a little water until the juice stops "working," meaning the fermentation has finished.

7. Tightly seal the barrels and let the cider mature, depending on the varieties and weather. It can take 3 to 6 months until the cider is ready to drink. Cheers!

We always look forward to the beginning of fall. Yes the weather gets colder and the days get shorter, but it's also when the apple season kicks in. And what could be cozier than a creamy rice pudding with some baked apples?

Nutmeg rice pudding with cider-baked apples

SERVES 6

3 cups [750 ml] whole milk

$7/8$ cup [200 ml] heavy cream

$3/4$ cup [150 g] short-grain rice

$1/2$ cup [100 g] superfine sugar

$1/2$ tsp freshly grated nutmeg

FOR THE CIDER-BAKED APPLES:

5 Tbsp [75 g] butter

$1/4$ cup [50 g] packed each light and dark brown sugar

$11/4$ cups [200 g] raisins or golden raisins

2 Tbsp honey

Finely grated zest of 1 small orange

Finely grated zest of 1 lemon

1 tsp ground allspice

1 tsp freshly grated nutmeg

$1/2$ tsp ground cinnamon

pinch ground cloves

6 small cooking apples, each weighing about 7 oz [200 g]

6 Tbsp [90 ml] fruity vintage cider

1. For the baked apples: Melt the butter, add both sugars, and stir until there are no lumps. Stir in the dried fruit, honey, orange and lemon zest, and spices and let go cold.

2. Preheat the oven to 375°F [190°C]. Remove the cores from the apples with a corer then open up the cavity further with a small, sharp knife until the holes measure $11/4$ in [3 cm] across. Take a small slice off the bottom if necessary so that they sit flat, then score a horizontal line through the skin around the middle of each one. Put them into a large baking dish and stuff the cavities with the fruit mixture. Pour the cider into the dish, cover loosely with foil, and bake for 30 minutes. Uncover and cook for 10 minutes more, or until they are soft to the center and lightly caramelized and the sauce is thick and bubbling.

3. Meanwhile, make the rice pudding. Put the milk, cream, rice, sugar, and nutmeg into a pan, bring to a boil, and simmer for 30 to 35 minutes, stirring regularly, until the rice is tender and the mixture is creamy. Rest for 5 to 10 minutes. Serve with the apples.

Or you could try...

Vanilla-roasted plums. Put $11/2$ lb [700 g] halved, pitted plums cut-side up in a shallow baking dish. Slit open 1 large vanilla bean, scrape out the seeds, and add them to $1/4$ cup [50 g] superfine sugar, then cut the bean into 4 pieces. Tuck the bean pieces in among the plums and scatter over the vanilla sugar. Drizzle over 3 Tbsp water and bake as before for 30 to 45 minutes until the plums are tender and the juices are thick and syrupy.

If you love baked apples and you love custard, you'll adore this recipe—it brings the two together beautifully. It's one of the only recipes we've come across that has a set custard inside. Genius!

Warm apple, honey & vanilla custard pie

SERVES 8 TO 10

FOR THE PIE DOUGH:

3 cups [350 g] all-purpose flour

Scant ½ cup [50 g] self-rising flour

Scant ½ cup [50 g] cornstarch

Large pinch salt

1¼ cups [275 g] chilled butter, cut into pieces

½ cup [100 g] superfine sugar

3 extra-large egg yolks, beaten together with 1 tsp vanilla bean paste and 2 Tbsp cold water

A little beaten egg, for sealing and brushing

2 Tbsp granulated sugar, for decoration

FOR THE FILLING:

2¾ lb [1.25 kg] dessert apples, such as Golden Delicious, peeled, cored, and thinly sliced

2 large free-range eggs, plus 2 extra yolks

¼ cup [100 g] honey

1 Tbsp self-rising flour

1 cup [250 ml] heavy cream

1 tsp vanilla bean paste

Extra cream or custard, to serve

1. Sift the flours, cornstarch, and salt into a food processor, add the butter, and whiz until the mix resembles fine bread crumbs. Stir in the superfine sugar and egg yolk mix and whiz briefly until it starts to stick together. Turn out onto a floured counter and knead briefly until smooth. Cut off a 11½-oz [325-g] piece, wrap it in plastic wrap, and set to one side.

2. Roll the remaining dough out thinly on a lightly floured counter into a 12-in [30-cm] disk and use to line a greased 9-in [23-cm] loose-bottomed tart pan, 1½ in [4 cm] deep, leaving the edges overhanging. Chill for 20 minutes. Knead the dough trimmings with the second piece of dough, wrap in plastic wrap, and chill alongside the pastry shell. Meanwhile, preheat the oven to 340°F [170°C].

3. Line the pastry shell with foil, cover with a thin layer of pie weights, and bake for 20 minutes. Remove the foil and weights and return to the oven for another 10 minutes until lightly golden. Let cool.

4. Put the sliced apples in a large mixing bowl. Whisk the eggs, yolks, honey, and flour in a pitcher until smooth, then whisk in the cream and vanilla paste. Pour over the apples and stir together well. Spoon the lot into the pastry shell, trying to make sure it's as level as possible and slightly domed in the center.

5. Reknead and roll out the remaining dough into a 10-in [25-cm] disk. Brush the edges with beaten egg, lift over the shell, and press the edges together to seal. Make a small hole in the lid's center, brush with egg, and sprinkle with granulated sugar. Bake for about 1½ hours, covering with foil once nicely browned, until the apples are tender when pierced with a skewer and the custard has set. Let cool for 30 minutes before serving.

This makes more jam than you need for one cake, but it'll keep in the refrigerator for a few weeks and is great stirred into yogurt, on scones or, of course, on hot buttered toast.

Or you could try ... Strawberry, rhubarb, and elderflower cake. Replace the raspberry jam with strawberry and rhubarb jam (see page 72). Whip the cream with 2 Tbsp elderflower cordial (see page 187). Mix scant 1 cup [100 g] powdered sugar with 4 tsp elderflower cordial and 1 to 1½ tsp warm water, spread over the top of the cake, and set before cutting.

Sponge cake with baked raspberry jam & lemon cream

SERVES 8

2 Tbsp [30 g] butter, melted and cooled,
plus extra for greasing

2 cups [190 g] all-purpose flour, plus extra for dusting

4 extra-large free-range eggs

1½ cups [300 g] superfine sugar

1 tsp baking powder

Pinch salt

Powdered sugar, for dusting

FOR THE BAKED RASPBERRY JAM:

4 cups [500 g] firm and really ripe raspberries

2½ cups [500 g] superfine sugar

2 tsp lemon juice

FOR THE LEMON CREAM:

⅞ cup [200 ml] fresh whipping or heavy cream

2 Tbsp powdered sugar

Finely grated zest of 1 small lemon

2 tsp lemon juice

1. For the jam: Preheat the oven to 350°F [180°C]. Spread the raspberries in a thin layer over the bottom of one medium ovenproof dish and the sugar in another. Pop them in the oven and bake for 30 minutes, until they are really hot but the fruit is still holding its shape. Quickly stir the sugar into the raspberries with the lemon juice, spoon into a bowl, and let cool, then cover and chill until needed.

2. Lightly grease two 9½-in [24-cm] sandwich pans with melted butter, line the bottoms with parchment paper, grease again, and then dust with flour, knocking out the excess. Increase the temperature to 375°F [190°C].

3. Separate the eggs into 2 large mixing bowls. Beat the yolks and sugar together for 2 minutes, then add 7 Tbsp [100 ml] warm water and whisk for another 10 minutes until thick and moussy. Sift the flour, baking powder, and salt together and gently fold in with a large spoon in 3 batches, then fold in the melted butter. Whisk the egg whites into soft peaks and gently fold in.

4. Pour the batter equally into the prepared cake pans and bake for 18 to 20 minutes until firm to the touch, golden, and just beginning to shrink away from the sides of the pans. Turn the cakes out immediately onto a wire rack, flip them over, and let cool.

5. To assemble the cake: Place one sponge top-side down onto a cake plate and spread with 6 to 8 Tbsp jam. Whip the cream with the powdered sugar, lemon zest, and juice into soft peaks and spread onto the base of the other. Flip over onto the top of the raspberry sponge and dust with powdered sugar.

We either eat this cake hot, straight from the oven, as a dessert with custard, or leave it to go cold to serve with cups of tea. Bring back elevenses, we say!

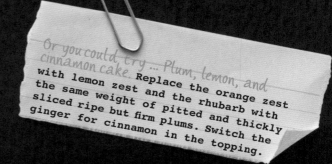

Or you could try ... Plum, lemon, and cinnamon cake. Replace the orange zest with lemon zest and the rhubarb with the same weight of pitted and thickly sliced ripe but firm plums. Switch the ginger for cinnamon in the topping.

Rhubarb, orange & hazelnut cake

SERVES 8 TO 10

8³⁄₄ oz [250 g] prepared rhubarb, cut into 4cm lengths

1³⁄₄ cups [350 g] superfine sugar

Finely grated zest and juice of 1 large orange

1¹⁄₃ cups [200 g] skinned hazelnuts

1¹⁄₄ cups [150 g] self-rising flour

1 tsp baking powder

1¹⁄₄ cups [300 g] unsalted butter, softened

4 large free-range eggs

FOR THE TOPPING:

3¹⁄₂ Tbsp [50 g] butter

¹⁄₄ cup [50 g] packed light brown sugar

¹⁄₂ tsp ground ginger

²⁄₃ cup [100 g] skinned hazelnuts, coarsely chopped

1. Mix the rhubarb with ¹⁄₄ cup [50 g] of the superfine sugar and half the orange zest. Cover and set aside for 20 minutes. Grease an 8-by-10-in [20-by-25-cm] shallow cake pan and line with parchment paper. Preheat the oven to 375°F [190°C].

2. Put the hazelnuts into a food processor and whiz until finely chopped. Add the flour and baking powder and whiz together until very finely ground.

3. Cream the butter, remaining sugar, and orange zest together until pale and fluffy. Beat in the eggs, one at a time, then fold in the hazelnut and flour mixture and 4 Tbsp of the orange juice. Spoon the batter into the prepared cake pan and level the surface, then spoon the rhubarb pieces evenly over the top. Bake for 25 minutes.

4. Meanwhile, for the topping, melt the butter in a small pan, then stir in the sugar, ground ginger, and hazelnuts and mix together well.

5. Remove the part-cooked cake from the oven and scatter the topping evenly over the top. Return the cake to the oven, reduce the oven temperature to 350°F [180°C], and bake for another 20 minutes, until a skewer inserted into the center of the cake comes away clean. Let cool in the pan, then remove and serve cut into squares.

The quince, once a favorite of the Victorian garden, has fallen slightly out of favor of late. But we're very fond of it. If you can't track them down, don't fret—firm pears or dessert apples such as russets or Cox's will do brilliantly.

Quince & ginger upside down pudding

SERVES 8

2 to 2¼ lb [900 g to 1 kg] quinces (about 4 to 5 large fruit)

Scant 1 cup [175 g] superfine sugar

¾ cup [170 g] unsalted butter

Scant 1 cup [100 g] all-purpose flour

2 tsp ground ginger

1 tsp ground cinnamon

¼ tsp ground cloves

¼ tsp freshly grated nutmeg

¼ tsp salt

¼ cup [50 g] packed light brown sugar

3 extra-large free-range eggs

1/3 cup [125 g] light corn syrup

1 Tbsp finely grated fresh gingerroot

1 tsp baking soda

1. Peel, quarter, and core the quinces, then cut them into ½-in [1-cm] thick wedges and drop them into a bowl of lemon water. Preheat the oven to 350°F [180°C].

2. Put the sugar and 4 Tbsp water into a large frying pan and dissolve over low heat. Bring to a boil and cook for 3 to 4 minutes until amber-caramel in color. Remove from the heat, add 3½ Tbsp of the butter, and swirl the pan until it has melted and mixed in.

3. Drain and dry the quinces, then add to the pan. Cook for 7 to 8 minutes, carefully turning now and then, until just tender when pierced with a knife. Using a slotted spoon, spoon the fruit over the bottom of a buttered, shallow, 9-in [23-cm] cake pan. Return the syrup to the heat and boil until reduced and thickened. Pour over the quinces and let cool.

4. Sift the flour, spices, and salt into a bowl. Beat the remaining butter in a bowl until pale and fluffy. Add the brown sugar and beat for 3 minutes, then gradually beat in the eggs. The mixture will curdle, but don't worry. Beat in the syrup and grated ginger, then gently mix in half of the flour mixture. Mix the baking soda with 2 Tbsp boiling water, beat into the batter then add the remaining flour. Pour over the quinces and bake for 15 minutes until the pudding is well-colored. Cover loosely with foil, lower the oven to 340°F [170°C], and cook for 25 to 30 minutes until a skewer pushed into the center of the cake comes out clean. Let the cake cool in the pan for 10 minutes, then turn out onto a serving plate and serve.

The gooseberry—another woefully underused fruit. Raw, they do seem a bit unpromising: hard, hairy, and face-scrunchingly sour. But when slowly cooked with sugar they really come into their own.

Gooseberry & lemon meringue pies

MAKES 8 INDIVIDUAL TARTS

FOR THE PIE DOUGH:

Scant 2 cups [225 g] all-purpose flour

¼ tsp salt

½ cup [65 g] powdered sugar

½ cup [125 g] chilled unsalted butter, cut into small pieces

1 extra-large free-range egg yolk, beaten together with 4 tsp ice-cold water

FOR THE FILLING:

6 cups [900 g] gooseberries, trimmed

Finely grated zest and juice of 1 lemon

¾ cup [150 g] superfine sugar

2 Tbsp cornstarch, mixed together with 2 Tbsp cold water

3 extra-large free-range egg yolks

3½ Tbsp [50 g] unsalted butter

FOR THE MERINGUE:

3 extra-large free-range egg whites

Scant 1 cup [175 g] superfine sugar

1. For the pie dough: Sift the flour, salt, and powdered sugar into a food processor. Add the butter and whiz until the mixture resembles fine bread crumbs. Add the egg yolk mix to the bowl and pulse briefly until it begins to stick together. Turn out onto a lightly floured counter and knead until smooth, then cut into 8 pieces and chill for 15 minutes. Thinly roll out the dough and use to line 8 buttered 4-in [10-cm] tart shells, 1½ in [4 cm] deep. Line the shells with foil and chill for another 15 minutes.

2. Preheat the oven to 400°F [200°C]. Fill the chilled tart shells with pie weights and bake for 15 minutes. Remove the foil and weights and bake for 3 to 5 minutes or until the bottoms are golden brown. Set aside.

3. Meanwhile, make the filling. Put the gooseberries in a pan with 2 Tbsp lemon juice and the sugar. Cover and simmer gently for about 15 minutes, stirring occasionally, until just tender. Tip into a strainer set over a pan to drain, then simmer the juice vigorously until reduced to about ⅞ cup [200 ml]. Stir the cornstarch mix in with the drained gooseberries and lemon zest and simmer for 2 minutes, stirring, until thick. Remove from the heat, cool slightly then stir in the egg yolks and butter. Spoon into the tart shells and let cool.

4. Reduce the temperature to 340°F [170°C]. Whisk the egg whites in a clean bowl into medium-stiff peaks, then whisk in the sugar 1 Tbsp at a time to make a stiff, glossy meringue. Spread it evenly over the tarts, then swirl with the tip of a knife. Bake for 15 minutes until lightly browned. Serve warm or cold.

This is a very clever recipe because you use the egg whites for the pavlova meringue and the yolks for the curd: very good housekeeping indeed. If you can't come by cobnuts, hazelnuts will be dandy.

Cobnut pavlovas with passion fruit curd

SERVES 4

5¼ oz [150 g] cobnuts in their shells or ¼ cup [40 g] shelled and skinned hazelnuts

3 extra-large, very fresh free-range egg whites

Pinch salt

Scant 1 cup [175 g] superfine sugar

1 tsp cornstarch

½ tsp white wine vinegar

⅝ cup [150 ml] heavy cream, lightly whipped, to serve

The pulp from 4 ripe and wrinkly passion fruit, to serve

FOR THE PASSION FRUIT CURD:

The pulp from 12 large, ripe and wrinkly passion fruit

3 extra-large free-range eggs, plus 3 extra yolks

3 extra-large free-range egg yolks

Scant 1 cup [175 g] superfine sugar

½ cup [120 g] unsalted butter

1. For the curd: Scoop the passion fruit pulp into a pan and bring to a gentle simmer. Take off the heat and stir for about 5 minutes, then tip into a strainer set over a bowl and rub out the juice with a wooden spoon. You should be left with about ⅞ cup [200 ml] juice.

2. Put the eggs, egg yolks, passion fruit juice, sugar, and butter into a heatproof bowl. Place over a pan of just simmering water and stir continuously for about 15 minutes until the curd has thickened and leaves behind a visible trail when drizzled back over the surface. Pour into two sterilized 12¼-oz [350-g] jars, cover with waxed jam disks, let cool, then seal. It will keep in the refrigerator for 3 to 4 weeks.

3. For the pavlovas: Preheat the oven to 400°F [200°C]. Spread the cobnuts onto a baking sheet and roast for 25 to 30 minutes or until crunchy. (Hazelnuts will only need 6 to 7 minutes.) Let cool, then chop coarsely. Lower the oven temperature to 275°F [140°C].

4. Whisk the egg whites in a large bowl with a pinch of salt into stiff peaks. Gradually whisk in the sugar, a spoonful at a time, to make a stiff and shiny meringue, then whisk in the cornstarch and vinegar. Stir in the chopped nuts.

5. Drop 4 large spoonfuls of the mixture onto 2 baking sheets lined with parchment paper and shape into 4-in [10-cm] circles with the back of the spoon, making a slight dip in the center. Bake for 40 to 45 minutes until pale. Turn off the oven and let them cool inside.

6. To serve: Spoon some of the whipped cream into the hollow of each pavlova, drizzle over some of the passion fruit curd, then spoon over the pulp. Serve immediately, before the meringue starts to go soft.

Recipe List

Breakfasty bits

Soups

Salads

Appetizers, snacks & light dishes

Main dishes—Veggie

Fishy

Birdy

Meaty

Desserts

Teatime treats

Breads

Preserves & cordials

Notes

Eggs are free-range and large unless otherwise stated; herbs are fresh; salt is sea salt, and pepper is freshly ground black pepper unless otherwise suggested. Use unwaxed lemons for grating and zesting. Spoon measures are level.

Anyone who is pregnant or in a vulnerable health group should avoid recipes that use raw egg whites or lightly cooked eggs.

Cooking times used are based on a conventional oven. If you are using a fan-assisted oven, set the temperature to 50°F to 59°F [10°C to 15°C] lower than called for in the recipe.

We believe that seasonal, locally produced food simply tastes better, so try and buy local wherever possible.

Index

Editorial director: Anne Furniss
Project editor: Simon Davis
Art direction & design:
Victoria Sawdon at Big Fish®
Photographer: Andrew Montgomery
Illustrator: Ariel Cortese at Big Fish®
Recipe consultant: Debbie Major
Props stylist: Jo Harris
Production: James Finan, Vincent Smith

First published in 2013 by
Quadrille Publishing Limited
Pentagon House
52–54 Southwark Street
London SE1 1UN
www.quadrille.com

Quadrille is an imprint of Hardie Grant
www.hardiegrant.com.au

Reprinted in 2016 (twice), 2017
10 9 8 7 6 5 4

Text © 2013 YEO VALLEY

Photography © 2013 Andrew Montgomery

Design and layout © 2013
Quadrille Publishing Limited

Cataloguing in Publication Data:
a catalogue record for this book
is available from the
British Library.

ISBN: 978 184949 732 9

Printed in China

Thank you

To Dad for giving us so much opportunity.

To Vicky for her patience, her beautiful design, and great creativity.
To Perry, Lee, and Ariel from Big Fish.
To Andrew for his fantastic photography.
To Debbie for her help with inspirational recipes and cooking.
To Anne and Simon from Quadrille for their experience and huge support.
To Tim and Sarah, Amanda and Phil, Mom, and all at Yeo Valley.

Lastly to Clive, Emily, Alice, William, and Maisie
for their loving and enthusiastic support.

This book, my first, has been a huge learning curve and a big team effort.
It's been brilliant—a huge thank you to everyone involved!